COME COOK WITH ME

Come Cook with Me

MAURICE BROCKWAY

Introduction by Pauline Trigère

ATHENEUM

New York

NOTE: I have sometimes used brand names
because they are my favorites, but the reader
may of course make substitutions.   M.B.

This book is for
E.J.D.
who enjoys food
even more than I do

PREFACE

While on a sabbatical from my duties as Banquet
Manager of New York's Sheraton-East Hotel, I took
a "cook's tour" of the French provinces in order to
experience first-hand the joys of dining where haute
cuisine was born.

One day after a superb luncheon in the garden of
the Hotel du Domino in Périgueux, suddenly I was
overwhelmed by a wave of nostalgia. I had enjoyed a
heady garlic soup, Poulet Grandmère aux Truffes
cooked to perfection, Soufflé Grand Marnier, and
Café Filtre.

Now I was sitting in a quiet corner of the garden,
enjoying a second cigarette and a moment of quiet
reflection. Surely the thought of more food could not
penetrate and surfeit this felicitous mood, yet somehow I was again ten years old, watching our beloved
cook Hettie prepare Chicken Fricassee in Grandmother's kitchen.

It was at that precise moment that I decided I
wanted to write this book, not only as a record to
enjoy myself, but to share with others.

I could actually smell the aroma of Hettie's biscuits wafting up from the oven, and I realized I had traveled a long distance on the pathway of gastronomic pleasures . . . from a little town in upstate New York and chicken with fricassee gravy to a little town in Le Périgord and chicken with truffles.

Intrigued by those mysterious black dots in the middle of the goose liver the first time I had ever tasted pâté de foie gras, here I was in the center of the most famous truffle-producing region in the world . . . thinking of fricassee gravy! It would have served me right had a pig come sniffing around me rather than the barren soil near the large oak trees, seeking out those exotic epicurean conceits.

But, compensation enough, I reflected that my appreciation of Chicken Fricassee was all the stronger because my tastes had become more sophisticated. Indeed, my visits to the font of haute cuisine served to inspire me in much the same way artists and designers are inspired by visits to Paris.

We Americans are most familiar with truffles in foie gras or atop Eggs Benedict, but the true aficionado knows many ways they can be enjoyed. As either appetizer or late supper, the classic combination is foie gras studded with truffles, spread on crusty French bread, and washed down with a properly chilled Dom Perignon. As we used to say in upstate New York, "That's eating, brother."

But "good eating," to use the vernacular, need not depend on such expensive repasts as Foie Gras aux Truffes and champagne, or Lobster Thermidor, or Oysters Rockefeller, or Chateaubriand with Béarnaise accompanied by a premier cru Château Lafitte Rothschild.

As I have traveled, I have learned, as I hope this book will bear witness, that the simplest foods properly and affectionately prepared can indeed be foods for the gods. Fried salt pork (and shudder not until you have tasted it), canned soup "doctored" with imagination, even popcorn can approach culinary heights when done well . . . and this of course means preparation as well as correct service, and, naturally, the proper occasion.

So come journey with me, and for luggage all you will require is a genuine love of good food and an interest in reading about it. Bon voyage; bon appétit!

INTRODUCTION

One of my great pastimes is to read cookbooks. I have a passion for them and own quite a collection. Reading in bed puts me delightfully to sleep while I savor —before dreaming of it—a rare exotic dish. Not unlike Proust in *Remembrance of Things Past* and his famous little "madeleine," I can almost visualize the life that is the background of the recipes I read. I call to mind those faraway lands that are home to so many ingredients . . . India and the pungent taste of ginger . . . the Gold Coast and the aroma of cocoa . . . Genoa—strong with basil . . . truffles from Périgord . . . my mind wanders to faraway places.

Now, what fun to get Maurice Brockway's book and follow him on his tour. Enjoy with him the old kitchen . . . in the old house . . . his marvelous cook Hettie, teaching him not to gobble but to enjoy the food. Take a trip with him to the South of France . . . enjoy the Bouillabaisse and Marseille . . . go with him to Bucks County, where life seems so genteel . . . and so neighborly.

Gourmet eating is pleasurable, to be sure. Analyzing a dish—how it is made, what is in it—is fine, but for me no cooking, no eating, can ever be separated from its environment. The beautifully appointed table . . . the candlelight . . . the congenial friends and guests, the understanding, the warm glow after the first glass of wine . . . Everything today tends to make cooking more attractive too—the kitchen decor, the cooking utensils, the gadgety ovens all are part of a beautiful life, and all for you to enjoy. "Come Cook with Me," says Maurice Brockway— and I say, "Avec plaisir."

Pauline Trigère

CONTENTS

COME COOK WITH ME

∽ I ∾

HETTIE AND UPSTATE
NEW YORK

I was brought up by my grandparents in a lovely old house in a small town located in upstate New York near the picturesque Thousand Islands and the Canadian border. Like most of our neighbors, we had a "hired girl" who did everything, but our Hettie's crowning achievements were in the kitchen.

Hettie was sixteen when she came to my grandparents long before I was born, and Grandmother always said: "She didn't know a parsnip from a parson then." However, after several years of patient training in the rudiments of cooking on the part of Grandmother—who was a "by ear" cook herself—this situation was altered favorably, and Hettie soon learned what had to be done to food to meet the exacting and knowledgeable standards of my grandfather.

Grandmother did a remarkable job, for Hettie, bless her, came to be a truly outstanding and, best of all, completely imaginative cook. She liked to cook, and that certainly is *the* essential requirement

3

toward becoming a good cook. Furthermore, she was not afraid to try an unusual touch here and there. A good cook must be a bit of a gambler, and even though you can't always win, the odds are surely in your favor if at least you try. And what's to lose?

Hettie was in her late twenties when I came along. She had a very big role in bringing me up, as my mother had died as a result of my birth. I am afraid that, because of this, I was pampered beyond belief by everyone in the family. Not by Hettie, however, as she could look on the family tragedy dispassionately. She was determined that I was not going to be spoiled, and I am forever grateful that she took a firm stand in refusing to give me my own way at every turn. She once gave me a spanking—my first— for disobeying her orders not to go away from the house without asking permission. I recall that I went to my room enraged, and stayed there sobbing most of the day. Hettie did not give in to my tantrum, but chose instead to ignore it. And wise she was, for the next day all was well between us, and I do not believe I ever disobeyed her again.

Hettie looked remarkably like a schoolteacher. Tall, very slender, and with a proudly erect carriage, she had long reddish-brown hair which she wore in a large figure-eight bun atop her head. Since her hair was naturally wavy, it was soft around her face. She wore a pince-nez with a gold chain and a loop over her ear, the glasses accentuating her high cheekbones and thin face.

In retrospect I now realize that Hettie sacrificed

4

any personal life she might have had to devote herself completely to our family and the house. She very
seldom even went to church on Sunday, as this was
the busiest day in the kitchen, but she never com-
plained.

Ours was a big house, the original part of it having
been built for his bride by my great-grandfather,
the leading carriage-maker in northern New York.
There was a portrait of him in the living room, and
when I was very young I always thought it was a
picture of one of the Smith Brothers of cough-drop
fame, for he had a long beard exactly like theirs.

One year Grandmother and Grandfather added a
conservatory to the already rambling old house;
then, a year later, a library; and, finally, a bed-
room wing to accommodate the ever expanding
weekend-guest list.

When it was decided to enlarge the kitchen, Hettie
held out for retaining the cookstove which burned
coal, insisting that she would never be able to cook
with electricity. When the new white-enameled electric range was installed, moreover, Hettie chose to
ignore it, as she was convinced she would be electro-
cuted if she so much as turned it on. Finally, Grandmother called the Niagara Power Company and
asked them to send out Miss Blank, their home-
economist demonstrator, to instruct Hettie in the
mysteries of the General Electric "monster." At the
end of the cooking demonstration Hettie not only
was enchanted with Miss Blank, General Electric,
and the Niagara Power Company, but she had made

plans to have the coal range moved to the summer kitchen to be used only in emergencies when the power lines might be out of order. The new stove could not improve Hettie's cooking technique, but it fascinated her so—especially the deep-well cooker —that for weeks we ate stews and pot roast until the novelty finally wore off.

Hettie did something to Chicken Fricassee that took it out of the realm of ordinary food and made it food for the gods. I asked her recently to tell me what it was, and, not surprisingly, she doesn't know. Her reply was: "I used to cut up the birds, put them in a kettle with some celery and onion, salt and pepper, and boil them slowly in enough water to cover." So far, so good; but I know she then invoked some sort of alchemy which certainly escaped me, the only member of the household then privileged and interested enough to spend a great deal of time in the kitchen. Part of the magic surely was the fact that the chickens were raised right on the property, then killed and dressed twelve hours before cooking.

It was not only Chicken Fricassee that had her special touch, but everything, including those huge biscuits awash with that golden-yellow fricassee gravy. Grandfather always served at table, and since I was forever ravenous he would serve my plate first—a large piece of white meat, a liver, two biscuit halves, mashed potatoes, and whatever vegetables were then at their peak in our garden. I was always ready for more chicken and biscuits before he had finished serving the rest of the family.

Hettie and Upstate New York

Hettie is Irish, and I am sure she brought a "wee one" with her from Ireland when she came to our house. There had to be some shenanigans in the bowl when Hettie made piecrust. It's true she used lard, which she "tried out" herself in a big iron kettle, but the delicate touch imparted to her flaky piecrust was something more than merely human. Hettie made all kinds of pies. Apple was probably my favorite, and in all my eating experience since, there have never been apple pies like those she used to bake.

Once in a while Hettie would make what she called MAPLE FRAPPE. I was delighted to help chop the ice which Tommy, the handyman, would get out of the big icehouse located out beyond the vegetable garden under a huge maple tree. Every winter, when the river was frozen, Grandfather hired a local man and his son to cut the large blocks of ice and haul them on a sleigh up the long hill to the icehouse. They were packed in sawdust from the lumber mill, and there they lasted all through the long hot summer. Each morning a large piece was dug out of the sawdust—which served as perfect insulation—washed with the hose, then put into the icebox in the summer kitchen. We were extremely advanced as we had a drain from the ice chest instead of the large pan everyone else seemed to use to catch the drippings.

I was delighted also to turn the freezer crank for the privilege of "licking" the ladle. Try this, and soon: 6 eggs beaten until creamy, 1 cup of pure maple syrup, 1 can of condensed milk, 1 can of evap-

7

Hettie and Upstate New York

orated milk, 1 pint of heavy cream whipped, and ½ teaspoon of salt. Mix together and freeze in an old-fashioned ice-cream freezer—not in the refrigerator ice trays. This makes 3 pints of frappe which, by itself is pure nectar, but atop warm apple pie is a delicacy that must be tasted to be believed.

On second thought, maybe you shouldn't even serve this unless you can't resist making big apple pies and turning the crank of the freezer. For I warn you, once your family and guests have tasted this rare treat, it will be a *must* forever more.

Spring and early summer were times of true eating pleasure, and Hettie went all out with fresh asparagus, rhubarb, new peas, and strawberries. Each spring we had at least one meal consisting of CREAMED FRESH ASPARAGUS. It was not cream-of-asparagus soup—it was the freshest small shoots of asparagus cut from our garden, cooked ever so quickly but gently in a small amount of water with salt and white pepper. Then, heavy cream generously poured over and just heated, never boiled. This was served in soup plates and accompanied by hot home-made bread. Dessert was usually fresh strawberries, washed and lightly sprinkled with sugar. Or it might be FRESH RHUBARB PIE. I don't think Hettie invented this pie, but she surely raised it to a level of perfection where nothing more could be desired.

For a 9-inch pie, use 4 cups of fresh rhubarb scraped and cut into 1-inch pieces, 1½ cups of sugar, 2 whole eggs, and a sprinkle of nutmeg. Mix all together thoroughly and pour into the lined pie

8

Hettie and Upstate New York

plate. Cover with the top crust. Wrap the edge with wet strips of gauze to prevent the juices from cooking out. Place in a hot oven (450°F.) for 10 minutes to set the crust, then reduce heat to 375° and continue baking for another 30 minutes. Cool on a rack. Do not refrigerate this or any other pie, because it causes the juices to soak into the crust.

Lemon pie was a once-a-week dessert at our house, and Hettie alternated between meringue and two-crust. I liked both very much, but now when I see what some cooks have done to lemon-meringue pie I cringe. Those 6-inch high meringues on commercial pies, all that marshmallow—ugh!—are overdoing it a bit.

Fortunately, no one has figured out a way to bas-tardize old-fashioned Two-Crust Lemon Pie, which is best served very cold. Thinly slice 5 lemons (skin and all), remove the seeds, put the slices in a bowl, and add 1½ cups of sugar, a pinch of salt, 1 table-spoon of tapioca, and 5 whole eggs slightly beaten. Mix well and put aside while you prepare the dough for the crusts. Then proceed as for the Rhubarb Pie.

Lemon pie

You do know how to make a Basic Piecrust, don't you? The recipe I use consists of 6 cups of all-purpose flour, 1½ teaspoons of salt, and 1 pound of chilled lard. Sift together the flour and salt and then, with your fingers, carefully work the flour into the lard until it is the size of many tiny peas. Then slowly add cold water (about ½ cup) and stir gently with a fork until the mixture clings together. Handle ever so gently and mold into a large ball. Refriger-

Pie Crust

ate for an hour. Then carefully break off a piece the size of a large snowball and roll it on a floured surface (marble is best) into a circle which will fit a 9-inch pie pan. Fold in half and lift gently into the pie pan, which has been lightly floured to prevent sticking. For a 2-crust pie, trim around the edge of the pan with a sharp knife, and save the scraps for the next crust.

Right here let me tell you about a lady who lives in Bucks County, Pennsylvania, who has perfected a piecrust recipe and an ingenious crust-rolling gadget that amateurs would do well to invest in. Her name is Manners Hammerstein, and she will send you an order blank for one of her pie-making kits if you write her at Sky Island, Upper Black Eddy, Pennsylvania. She has been on television many times demonstrating this method, a wonderful boon for the bride whose husband longs for pie like Mother used to make. I personally have tried Mrs. Hammerstein's method, and it's as "easy as pie."

Making excellent piecrust is most often the result of experience, and getting the "feel of the dough" from the time you start with the lard and flour. After adding the cold water, you must learn to shape and roll it, and it will help if you pretend you are handling the most fragile soap bubble, so obviously you must not have a "heavy hand."

If you are making a pie shell for lemon-meringue, cream, or chiffon pie, after you fit the crust into the pan do not trim until you have fluted the edge, using the thumbs and index fingers of both hands. Then trim carefully. Before putting the shell into the oven (temperature 425°F., then reduced to 375°, as with all pies), prick the crust in several places with a fork, cut a piece of aluminum foil to fit the bottom of the crust, and cover both with a layer of dry navy beans to hold the crust in place and prevent air bubbles. Carefully remove the beans and foil when the crust is partly cooled, and save the beans in a small jar for use over and over.

Back home, at the end of June, the local church held its annual Ice Cream Social, for which ladies of the parish made huge freezersful of ice cream, and marvelous cakes. One cake always especially intrigued me, because it was as delicious as it was easy to make. Mrs. Feistel's own recipe for her CHOCO-LATE CAKE tells us to mix together:

In a sifter—

> 1 cup granulated sugar
> 1½ cups all-purpose flour
> 3 tablespoons cocoa
> 1 level teaspoon soda
> pinch of salt

In a mixing bowl—

> 1 cup sour milk
> 3 tablespoons melted butter
> 1 egg yolk
> 1 tablespoon vanilla

Combine and bake at 375°F. in a well-greased 13 × 9-inch rectangular pan for about 20 minutes.

Mrs. Feistel's simple UNCOOKED FROSTING results

11

Frosting

from beating together, until it peaks, 1 egg white, ½ cup of light corn syrup, a pinch of salt and ½ teaspoon vanilla.

There was never any feeling of competition at these socials, but nevertheless all the good cooks tried to outdo themselves, and praise was eagerly sought. Grandmother always made several pounds of her special DIVINITY FUDGE, which was usually sold by advance order even before the "fancy table" was open to the public. This is especially good at Christmas, and here is how she made it.

Candy

Combine:

  3 cups extra-fine granulated sugar
  ½ cup white corn syrup
  ¾ cup water
  ¼ teaspoon salt
  ½ teaspoon cream of tartar
  6 egg whites
  2 cups chopped pecans, walnuts, or pistachios
  ½ teaspoon vanilla

Cook over a low flame until a drop forms a soft ball in cold water (or 250° on candy thermometer). Be careful it does not scorch. Have ready the egg whites beaten very stiff. Quickly pour the sugar syrup into the egg-white mixture, beating constantly at high speed. Remove the bowl from the beater, add the vanilla and the chopped nuts. Fold in, and pour onto a large platter or a piece of marble. When it is cool, cut it into 3 long strips and shape each into a long roll. Wrap each in waxed paper and put in a

potatoes or dumplings w
gr. peas

cold place (not the refrigerator) for 12 hours. Then
cut into ½-inch slices. This makes about 2 pounds of
candy.

Grandfather prided himself on always having new
peas for lunch on every July 4. They had to be
picked, shelled, and cooked within the space of one
hour.

Usually we had tiny new potatoes which were
cooked in a scant amount of water with a dash of
salt, then added to the peas. Hettie used to dig into
the side of the potato hill with a trowel, stealing a
few here and there, but being careful not to disturb
the plant itself. She always carefully patted the soil
back into place so that the remaining tubers would
continue to grow undisturbed. Other times we had
the fresh peas cooked with tiny dumplings, cream
added after the dumplings and peas were cooked.

We were lucky enough to have a miniature golf
course, tennis courts, and one elaborate croquet
set-up, plus a baseball diamond complete with a
team which Grandfather paid to play each weekend,
so it was something like living at a country club.
There were always weekend guests who supposedly
came for the various sports, but Hettie knew, and so
did I, that they were really there for the food, which
was served lavishly three times a day.

Sunday was the only time during the week when
the entire family had breakfast together. Today we
call this type of meal "brunch," a word I much
dislike but manage to live with and even use, as do
many people who want to describe a menu which at

potatoes

peas
dumplings
cream

13

our house could include: Grilled Baby Lamb Chops with Watercress; or Broiled Country Ham Steaks with Potatoes au Gratin; or, for a cold winter Sunday, Thick Sour-Cream Pancakes with Butter, Homemade Sausages, and Maple Syrup.

Always hot breads and Grandfather's favorite—Rhode Island Johnny Cake—were served. And frequently a deep-dish pie or a fruit cobbler, or many times hot homemade fried cakes as large as raised doughnuts.

And coffee. Here again the leprechauns must have been in the grinder or the pot, for there never was such coffee at any other time or place. I can taste it now, and I wish I knew the secret. Hettie preferred the boiled type settled with eggshells, but when Grandmother introduced her to the electric percolator it made no difference to Hettie. The coffee was still the best ever brewed. It just had to be some sort of Irish magic. I now use a Chemex filter, and find it the next-best method ever devised.

Hettie never approved of iced tea, but that did not stop her from making the best iced tea ever. She made it with green tea, and that alone was daring. But be daring, and try it that way the next time you serve iced tea.

Along about October 15 was pig-butchering time, during which the men would come early in the morning to set up the equipment and start the fires under the big iron kettle. Grandmother always went on a shopping tour that day, and I was sent to school early.

14

Hettie and Upstate New York

Hettie—not so squeamish—was in her glory when the pigs were cut up, and her day was made when she had the kettle on, "trying out" the lard. It had to be done slowly, for "too much heat ruins the texture," so it sometimes took a full week to complete the process, but the resulting product was of the highest quality, so all the effort was, to her, very worthwhile.

She always made a lot of cornmeal mush, to which she added the cracklings left from the lard, and a little sage. Then the mixture was packed into bread pans and covered with a thin layer of melted lard. The tins were put in the cold cellar and brought out one at a time for breakfast on cold mornings. The "scrapple" was sliced and fried, then served with home-cured bacon.

Hettie always "pickled" the bacon and hams, and they were sent to a smokehouse at a nearby farm. Hettie went out once to make sure the farmer was using only apple wood for the smoking. When she found acorns in the smokehouse, the poor hired man was certainly given a piece of her Irish mind.

I am reminded now that there is a place where this kind of ham and bacon is still made. I frequently send to the Bemis Market in Adams Center, New York, for the best ham anywhere in the world, and the bacon is second only to real Irish bacon. Send a check for $15.00 to Mr. Bemis and ask him to ship you one of his hams and a pound or two of bacon. He bones them before shipping, so they are easy to manage. Slice half of the ham and fry it in a skillet. The

15

aroma will probably drive you mad. Make a cream gravy, and then thank your lucky stars that you are alive. Don't boil the remainder. Put it, instead, in a roaster, stick it full of cloves, rub dark-brown sugar into it after you have scored it, and pour a large bottle of Coca-Cola into the pan. Roast slowly with the cover on for 1 hour at 325°F. Then uncover and continue roasting for ½ hour, basting at 10-minute intervals. And let's hear no more, please, about Virginia ham.

Early in November the Fortnightly Club had its annual open house, card party, and buffet supper. Since Grandmother was the perennial president as well as the proud possessor of Hettie, it was always voted at the June meeting to hold the party at our house.

Hettie would scarcely have recovered from Election. You see, my grandfather was on the Election Board and had been for most of his adult life. There were no voting machines then, so when the polls closed the committee took off their coats, lighted their cigars, and started counting the ballots. This was all taken very seriously in those days, and there were checks and double checks to make sure that the Republican candidates had won. (Ours was a strongly Republican township.) No drinking was allowed, due to Prohibition, but hard-cider eggnog was a tradition; and since the only important Democrat owned the only cider mill in town, it would have been considered partisan to refuse to drink the eggnog.

16

Along about nine o'clock Hettie would move into the Town Hall, where the counting of ballots took place. She came bearing kettles of steaming oyster stew and big bowls of oyster crackers. It was her shining hour, and she would go home to bed at midnight surely the happiest girl in America. Not one drop of oyster stew was ever left over, and the praises were high indeed.

The preparation for the Fortnightly Club's open house was a major production, despite the fact that the menu was always the same, having been arrived at years before through trial and trial. It consisted of Creamed Chicken with Hot Biscuits, Ham Loaf with Cheese Sauce, Molded Fruit Salad and— always the pièce de résistance—Miniature Pumpkin Pies with Whipped Cream, and Coffee.

Since well over one hundred persons attended each year, including the husbands, there were miniature pumpkin pies on every shelf in our house. Hettie insisted on making them all on the day of the party, and she planned two for each man. She even had special muffin tins used only for this one time each year. The pumpkin was not out of a can, either, but from our garden, boiled and sieved as needed. It was work, but well worth it. The guests wandered out into the crisp November night full of the joy of living. And full of delicious food, too. Hettie retired at three or four in the morning after every dish was washed and put away and her alarm clock set for 6:00 a.m. "to get the Boss's coffee made on time."

Plum pudding was much too English for Hettie,

Suet Pudding

but often in winter she made SUET PUDDING. Because
I very much disliked raisins, she always made two
puddings—one with and one without. Hettie would
use only the whitest beef-kidney suet thoroughly
chilled and then ground in the food chopper, using
the coarse blade.

Combine:

>¾ *cup ground suet*
>½ *cup dark molasses*
>½ *cup brown sugar*
>¾ *cup milk*

In another bowl sift together:

>1½ *cups flour*
>1½ *teaspoons baking powder*
>½ *teaspoon salt*
>1 *teaspoon cinnamon*
>½ *teaspoon nutmeg*

Also:

>1 *cup seeded raisins,*
>   *separated and dusted with flour*

Mix all ingredients together and pour into a well-
buttered pudding mold. Steam for 3 hours in a covered kettle of water. There will be plenty for 6 people.

My pudding was made the same way except that no
raisins were added. Usually the puddings were
served with hard sauce flavored with rum and
brandy.

Another great favorite of mine was a dessert
called (ridiculously, I always thought) APPLE CROW'S

NEST. I understand that the same dessert bears equally foolish names in various parts of the country, but, by whatever name, it still remains one of my favorites, and I serve it frequently here in Bucks County.

Hettie pared and cut in slices 8 or 10 pie apples, to which she added 1 very generous cup of light-brown sugar, the juice of 1 lemon, and 1 teaspoon of grated lemon rind mixed with 1 tablespoon of ground nutmeg. This mixture was put in a deep baking dish and then dotted with butter. Finally it was covered with a rich biscuit dough and baked for 45 minutes in a 350°F. oven. I make it now by using 2 cups of Bisquick, ¼ cup of sugar, ½ teaspoon of nutmeg, 3 tablespoons of melted butter, and 1 cup of milk. This is a rather thin batter, but it works perfectly. It makes generous servings for 6.

Apple Crow's Nest is always served with VINEGAR SAUCE, and when I was a youngster I would not eat any of the apples—only the topping aswim in hot Vinegar Sauce. To make this sauce, mix 1 cup of granulated sugar with 3 tablespoons of cornstarch, then add 3 cups of hot water and cook over a medium flame until clear and thickened. Remove from the stove, add ½ cup of cider vinegar, 1 teaspoon of ground nutmeg, and a very generous piece of butter. Keep warm over hot water until ready to serve. Excuse me while I slice some apples. Incidentally, I now eat huge portions of this dessert—apples and all. And I am reminded that when I was growing up I never ate whipped cream. It made me "seasick." I wish it still did.

spinach Salad

Hettie was ingenious, and frequently invented dishes. One day, for example, two ladies stopped by unexpectedly to visit, and since it was lunchtime Grandmother went to the kitchen to see if Hettie could prepare something "light" that they could eat out on the piazza.

Hettie, being from the Ould Sod, was extremely fond of greens, and the evening before we had had fresh spinach. There was still a goodly amount of it cold in the refrigerator. Hettie went to the garden and picked two cucumbers and a handful of scallions. She then cut the cooked spinach a bit, added diced cucumbers, chopped scallions, sliced hard-boiled eggs, cider vinegar, salt and pepper. This COLD SPINACH SALAD was served with cold baked ham sliced thin, and hot biscuits. There was home-made ice cream and red raspberries (Grandmother's favorite of all) and some of the famous iced green tea. Now you know what to do with that leftover spinach, or Swiss chard, or—especially delicious—dandelion greens.

The VANILLA ICE CREAM just mentioned was the only kind Hettie would make (other than the rather special Maple Frappe). For this she used 12 egg yolks beaten well, 1½ cups of sugar mixed with 3 heaping tablespoons of cornstarch, then blended with the eggs. Place the mixture in the top of a large double boiler, add 1 quart of milk and 1 quart of cream. Cook until the mixture coats the spoon; add ½ teaspoon of salt and a vanilla bean. Set aside to cool. Remove the vanilla bean. Freeze in a hand-turned 6-quart freezer. Not only is it much more fun than using the electric model, which Hettie would never even consider using, but you "get the feel of the cream" by the way the crank turns.

MINCEMEAT at our house was just that: the genuine article. It did not come from a package to which tap water had to be generously added, nor from a jar clearly stating on the label "Brandied." No, our mincemeat was authentic, and it took at least two full days to concoct.

To prepare 4 gallons of mincemeat you will need:

5 pounds lean beef (chuck or bottom round)
2 teaspoons salt
12 whole cloves
1 cracked nutmeg
a few pieces of cinnamon bark and whole allspice
½ gallon cider
2 pounds beef-kidney suet
1 peck Cortland (or other cooking) apples
1 pound raisins
1 pound currants
1 pound chopped citron peel
½ pound candied lemon peel
½ pound candied orange peel
2 teaspoons each of
  ground cinnamon
  ground cloves
  ground nutmeg
  ground allspice
3 pounds dark-brown sugar
1 cup molasses
1 pint brandy or sherry

First, the beef was seared in an iron Dutch oven. Then the salt was added, along with a small gauze bag in which were placed the cloves, nutmeg, cinnamon bark, and allspice. Enough cider was poured in to cover the meat, then the lid was put in place, and the whole thing was boiled very slowly for 3 or 4 hours until the meat was fork-tender.

The beef was allowed to cool in the pot overnight, then it was chopped (never ground) in a big wooden bowl using a 2-blade chopper. The cider in which it had cooked was reserved. Next, the suet, which had been kept ice-cold, was chopped. The beef and suet were mixed together in a large pot, and then the apples were peeled, cored, chopped, and added. Also the seeded raisins, currants, and chopped citron peel. Hettie made her own candied lemon and orange peel (grapefruit, also, which was my favorite, but which was not used in the mincemeat). The lemon and orange peel was cut up in small dices and added, and the ground cinnamon, cloves, nutmeg and allspice were put in. Then the cider in which the beef had cooked, plus enough additional cider to make ½ gallon. The mixture was cooked very slowly (stirred frequently to avoid sticking) for about 2 to 3 hours. Then the brown sugar and molasses were added. After another ½ hour of carefully watched cooking (and a great deal of stirring with a big wooden spoon), it was removed from the fire and cooled overnight. In the morning a pint of Grandfather's best brandy was stirred in before the mincemeat was placed in a large stone crock and packed down gently. If Grandfather had gone to his office early, in-

stead of the brandy—which he kept locked up—a
pint of Amontillado sherry was poured over the top
before a cover of several thicknesses of cheesecloth
was tied on and the lid put in place. It was ready
then and there for about 15 pies, but usually it was
allowed to ripen for two or three weeks, and if the
brandy supply was not depleted, it was given one or
two good splashes in the interval. A lot of time and
trouble? Yes, but compare this genuine mincemeat
with the packaged variety, and let your taste buds be
the final judge of whether the effort was worth it.

Hettie had many friends, but Irene Depew in particular always intrigued me. Her claim to fame was
not simply that she was a fabulous cook, but that she
was also the granddaughter of a woman who had
been Chef de Cuisine for Madame de Feriet, a member of the exiled French court, many of whom came
to northern New York via Canada and settled there.
Count Leray de Chaumont, Count Vincent de Rosiere,
and Joseph Bonaparte each had a town named in
his honor. Deferiet, New York, is a prosperous,
though small, paper-mill town still very much on the
map of Jefferson County.

Hettie acquired many pointers from her friend
Irene, but the one I recall most vividly was her way
with FLOATING ISLAND. I have never seen anyone prepare it quite this way, and as a youngster it was one
of my favorite desserts.

For the meringue "Island": beat until stiff 4 egg
whites flavored with 2 teaspoons of vanilla extract.
Then mix together ½ cup of sugar, 2 tablespoons of
arrowroot powder, and a pinch of salt. Stir this

quickly into 2 cups of boiling water, stirring and cooking until clear and thickened. Now fold the hot mixture into the egg whites, carefully but thoroughly. Rinse 8 individual molds with ice water, fill them with the mixture, and allow them to get very cold in the refrigerator.

For the custard: heat 2½ cups of milk in a double boiler, then mix together 1 cup of sugar, 3 tablespoons of cornstarch, and ½ teaspoon of salt, and add this combination to the milk. Cook until the mixture coats the spoon. Beat 4 egg yolks, adding 3 or 4 spoonfuls of the custard mixture to the yolks at first, and then stir the whole thing together. Remove from the heat and add your choice of lemon or vanilla extract (2 teaspoons). Or try it sometime with 1 teaspoon of rosewater and 1 teaspoon of almond extract. Strain through a fine sieve, cover, and chill.

When ready to serve, place 4 or 5 tablespoons of the custard into each "nappy" (a small individual glass bowl), unmold the "Island" into the center of the custard, and sprinkle with toasted slivered almonds. This will serve 8, but you had better plan on seconds.

Grandfather despised meat loaf; but occasionally he had to be away overnight on business and Hettie frequently took this opportunity to make a VEAL LOAF. Of course she insisted on grinding the veal (twice).

> *2 pounds ground veal*
> *½ pound ground pork*
> > *(mostly lean with a little fat)*

24

Hettie and Upstate New York

2 cups bread cubes
1 cup evaporated milk
2 chopped onions
2 tablespoons butter
salt and pepper
a pinch of savory
2 whole eggs
½ pound chicken livers
several strips salt pork

The bread cubes were soaked in the evaporated milk; the onions chopped and sautéed in the butter, salt, pepper, and savory with the eggs; and, finally, the raw chicken livers, dipped in bread crumbs, were put through the food grinder. She mixed all of this into the ground veal and pork with her hands to be sure it was well blended, and then packed it into a thoroughly greased bread pan. Very thin strips of fat salt pork were placed on top, and the loaf was baked for one hour in a 350°F. oven.

The MUSHROOM SAUCE: Put ½ pound of fresh mushrooms through a food grinder, using the coarse blade, then sauté them in ½ cup of butter over a hot flame. Add 1½ tablespoons of flour, stir well and add 1 cup of chicken stock and 1 cup of light cream; then a sprinkle of nutmeg and cook until slightly thickened.

Serve to 8 guests with a pilaf of rice and fresh green peas in butter. (This meat loaf is also delicious served cold.)

Once in a while on a cold night in winter when the

Salt Pork / cream gravy

thermometer had dropped to fifteen or twenty degrees *below* zero, Hettie would conjure up a dish which we all loved, as unlikely as it might sound to gourmets: FRIED SALT PORK WITH CREAM GRAVY. The lean salt pork was sliced, put into a skillet, and barely covered with cold water. Placed on the fire, it was allowed to come to a boil, then drained. The pork slices were wiped dry and dipped in flour lavishly seasoned with freshly ground pepper. A small amount of butter was heated in the skillet, and the pork slices were then fried slowly until well browned and crisp. If too much fat accumulated, it was poured off as the cooking proceeded. The meat was kept hot in the warming oven.

The CREAM GRAVY was made in the pan after the meat was all cooked. Add 4 heaping tablespoons of flour to 8 tablespoons of the fat in the pan and blend over a hot flame. Have ready 4 cups of half-milk-half-cream which have been heated to the boiling point. Remove the skillet from the stove and add the hot milk (so that it will not boil over), then return to the stove and stir over a low flame until thickened.

With this Hettie served potatoes which had been boiled in their jackets (the jackets removed while hot before serving) and cauliflower au gratin. Of course the freshly grated horseradish from our root cellar was a *must* with this, and, no matter how she tried, Hettie never seemed to cook enough salt pork.

Once in a while I was able to coax Hettie into making my favorite chocolate cake. The recipe was from Helen Gorman, the only girl in town who had

26

attended Foxcroft, and who lived in the mansion
built by the founders of our town. Helen had a flair
with everything she touched, and although this cake
was great, it was one of her lesser accomplishments.
I wish I knew what "Dunican" meant, as this was
called Helen Gorman's DUNICAN CAKE. I recently
came upon the recipe in my ten-year-old handwrit-
ing just as Helen gave it to me long ago.

"Into ¼ cup of butter blend 1 cup of sugar, add ½
cup of boiling water, ¼ cup of sour cream to which
has been added 1 teaspoon of soda. Stir in 1 whole
egg. Add 1 cup of sifted flour, 2 heaping tablespoons
of Dutch-process cocoa, and 1 teaspoon of vanilla.
Bake in two 9-inch pans, which have been well
greased and floured, in a 375°F. oven. The layers are
thin, so be careful not to overbake, as the cake
should be moist."

The filling is made with 1 generous cup of milk,
the yolk of 1 egg, ½ cup of sugar blended with 1
tablespoon of cornstarch and 1 heaping tablespoon
of cocoa. Cook in a double boiler until thickened.
Add ½ teaspoon of vanilla. Cool. Put between the
two layers of the cake. Ice the top only with a vanilla
icing. I have just stopped writing to make a Dunican
Cake. Why don't you stop reading and try it? If
Betty Crocker could get this into a package, she
would surely go down in culinary history.

I almost forgot to tell you about the NORTHERN
NEW YORK BAKED BEANS, at which Hettie was the
acknowledged master. (Incidentally, I have since
learned from Don Badertscher, whose family live in

X Baked Beans

Beans

Lorain, Ohio, that beans are also baked this way in Ohio, a state that seems to have a great deal in common, food-wise, with upper New York State.)

The dry marrow beans (2 pounds) were soaked overnight after having been washed and picked over carefully. In the morning they were boiled gently in the water in which they had soaked. As soon as they started to boil, a generous piece of salt pork was added to the pot, together with 2 medium-size onions, which had been cut up, and a healthy dash of black pepper.

The beans were boiled until tender, a little water being added if necessary (but they should not be awash). Remove from the stove and add 1½ cups of granulated sugar. Place in a baking pan, slice the boiled salt pork and arrange over the top. Bake in a 350°F. oven for about 1½ to 2 hours. Serve hot or cold to 8 or 10 eager eaters. I have discovered that if one does not have salt pork, a generous cup of mayonnaise added before baking produces wonderfully flavored beans. And I am sure you must know about bean sandwiches. Well, this is the way to bake the beans for anyone who really likes them.

About twenty miles away from where we lived was the Perch Lake Cheese Factory where only Limburger was made. Grandfather knew the old German man who ran the factory, so about once a month we would drive there and buy several large bricks of his delicious cheese. It was a great treat for me. The spotlessly clean workroom had the air of a hospital's operating theater, and smelled of heated milk and

28

whey. Summer and winter this area was always very warm, and it was a relief to go with Hans into the cave where the cheeses were aging—a natural cave running deep into a rocky hillside. Water from natural springs dripped down the walls and ran off in shallow trenches dug into the floor. The dampness was all-important to the proper curing of the cheese, which was arranged on countless shelves all around the "room." Every day each brick of cheese was given a rubdown with salt and moved to the next shelf, and since there were hundreds of bricks I marveled that one old man had the time and patience to repeat this procedure seven days a week.

Grandfather selected his cheese from the six-weeks-old shelf, and he always bought one for me from the two-weeks-old department. Actually it was more like curd at this stage, but it had a definite flavor and faint aroma of the more matured.

Sunday night was the Limburger cheese time, and I felt really grown-up when Grandfather and I would each have a slice or two of our cheese with crackers. I ate more mustard than cheese, and no amount of Grandfather's encouragement ever convinced me to eat the cheese sans moutarde as he did.

Now I serve a LIMBURGER SANDWICH which is extremely popular with most guests. I slice thinly several Italian red onions and marinate them for 3 hours in oil and vinegar seasoned with garlic and fennel. On a slice of pumpernickel bread I put a generous amount of Limburger cheese, then a layer of onions, topped with another—well-buttered—

slice of pumpernickel. Serve these with very cold beer for lunch on a hot day.

We must push on now to other people, other times, and other foods, but do reread this section later and see if you don't want to try everything Hettie did so superbly. I should not use the past tense, of course, for Hettie is very much alive and can still cook like the Irish angel that she is.

⌐ II ⌐

BUCKS COUNTY

I spent an exciting twelve years as Banquet Manager and Director of Sales, first at New York's Hotel Plaza (which I refer to as the last outpost of gracious living in America), then at the staid old Ambassador Hotel at Park Avenue and 51st Street. Its name was unfortunately changed to the Sheraton-East, but now it is gone from the scene, a victim of what is called "urban renewal." During this period I bought an old stone house built *circa* 1730 in Carversville, Solebury Township, Bucks County, Pennsylvania. It was to be a weekend retreat from the hectic pace of Manhattan, and it was just that for a year. During this period I raced down here each Friday night and back to town on Monday morning.

Soon, however, the peace and quiet, and friendly townspeople and charming neighbors, and the beauty of the countryside became a lure too hard to resist. At the same time Manhattan had become a complete bore—exasperating, enervating, frustrating—so I took the big step, resigned my enviable position at the hotel, and moved lock, stock, and twenty-two barrels to the country on a permanent basis.

I have lived in many parts of the United States and spent considerable time in France and Italy (the latter my favorite foreign country), but never before have I been fortunate enough to live in any place as friendly as Bucks County. There is an extraordinary rapport among the "natives" (I have met only one adult who was actually born in Bucks County), and as water seeks its own level, so do compatible people always seem to find one another —which is abundantly true here in Bucks County.

Bucks County, Pennsylvania, is much more than an area of land edging the Delaware River. It is more a state of mind than a way of life. Founded by William Penn in 1682 and named for Buckinghamshire in England, like its namesake it is called affectionately and intimately "Bucks."

English Quakers settled here in Lower Bucks and started building beautiful stone houses about 1700. Prior to this they had made do with quickly built log houses. The Pennsylvania Dutch (Germans) took over the upper part of the county and developed the rich farmland.

For an area the size of Bucks—which is roughly forty miles long and fifteen to twenty miles wide—to be so well known tells much about its inhabitants.

New Hope, a small village on the Delaware, was until 1900 just that—a small village on the Delaware. Then artists from New York and Philadelphia began to arrive, and in short order the town became a lively art center. Despite having been sadly commercialized, it has somehow managed to retain much of its original charm. Gradually the entire county became an artists' colony, then the theater people started buying houses and farms. At one point anyone who did not live near a celebrity was considered persona non grata.

Moss Hart bought a lovely stone house, and from his experiences in renovating it came the idea which later developed into the hit play and movie *George Washington Slept Here.*

We know for certain that George did sleep in Bucks County, as it was here that he crossed the Delaware on Christmas night 1776, moving downriver to Trenton, where he routed the British.

Dressed in an authentic Revolutionary uniform, each Christmas nowadays St. John Terrell, owner of the famous Music Circus in Lambertville, New Jersey, crosses the Delaware at the original site as thousands of people gather at Washington's Crossing, Pennsylvania, and Washington's Crossing, New Jersey, to watch the reenactment of this famous boat ride.

New York is only two hours away and Philadelphia only one, so many residents of the county commute daily to one place or the other. Many others maintain homes here and come down weekends only.

Winter is as delightful as summer, and although the diminished number of tourists does not please the owners of the many antique and gift shops, it does give the natives a chance to enjoy the county

3

quietly. Bucks County abounds in fine restaurants, most of which remain open throughout the year, as do the motels.

Entertaining at home is done on a large scale. Invitations arrive frequently, and in winter open house is more or less the rule each weekend. Progressive dinners are again a most popular way of entertaining, as they give weekend houseguests a chance to see some of the attractive homes, at the same time not putting a burden on any one host or hostess. Everyone is unusually considerate, for all appreciate these fine old houses. The women even refrain from wearing spike heels, which can be rough on random-width pine floors. Casual dress is the vogue, and both men and women wear whatever is most comfortable and easiest to get about in.

Word soon got around that I was fascinated by food and loved to cook. No one down here said, "Oh, I could never invite *you* to dinner," as they frequently had done in New York. There are no inhibited hostesses in Bucks County, and how fortunate for me, as I have learned a great many tricks and coaxed recipes from quite a few of my new friends. I would like to share some of them with you.

Helen Nickel and her daughter Janet Harvan have an excellent antique shop and decorating studio in nearby Lahaska. The two of them, with their husbands, share a magnificent old stone house in Ambler. I have been their guest many times, and Helen has given me some of her choice family recipes.

Having frequently told me about the POTATO

FILLING FOR TURKEY which she learned from her husband's mother, Helen was quick to volunteer the recipe when she learned that I was writing this book. Like all good cooks, she impressed upon me that this recipe is merely basic, and that she was not too sure about the amount of bread, as the size of loaves varies so much these days. To ensure that we would give the right proportions in this book, she said, "Come over on Thursday and I will stuff and roast a turkey for dinner so you can see for yourself exactly how I do it and what it tastes like." Just how far can one go for a friend's book?

For a 20-to-25-pound turkey, Helen boils 5 pounds of white potatoes (peeled) in salted water until they are fork-tender. She drains them and breaks them up gently with a fork (do not rice or mash). Then she sautés 2 pounds of chopped onions in ¼ pound of oleomargarine, mixes the potatoes and onions together while still hot, and adds 3 eggs, salt, pepper, and poultry seasoning to taste. Helen uses 2 standard-size loaves of day-old bread, which she dips in water, squeezes gently, and breaks up into the potato-onion mixture. She boils the neck and giblets in sufficient water to cover, adding salt and pepper, and when they are cooked she reserves the stock, and chops and adds the neck and giblets to the stuffing. The reserve stock is kept in the refrigerator while the bird is roasting, then the fat which has risen to the top is removed, the remainder being added to the pan juices to make a delicious gravy. Helen warns us to avoid packing the stuffing into the bird, as it swells even more than regular stuffing.

The Pennsylvania Dutch originated this as a filling for the Christmas goose, and it is still always used this way around Allentown and especially in Lancaster, Pennsylvania. The "plain people," as the Amish call themselves or are called, use hot mashed potatoes, but Helen Nickel's method of just breaking up the potatoes with a fork gives a much better consistency to the filling. It's just the greatest ever, and you may find you want to increase the amounts as Helen often does so she can bake an extra pan of the stuffing to reheat and serve with the left-over turkey.

In the soup section you will find Helen's recipe for Cream-of-Green-Tomato Soup which is extraordinarily good. And her method of preparing FRIED TOMATOES WITH CREAM GRAVY is so simple, yet so unusually delicious, that I have asked her to share it also.

Use only firm but ripe tomatoes, which are cut in half, unpeeled, and the stem end cut out. Dip them into flour which is seasoned with salt to taste and black pepper. An electric frying pan is best, for it has controlled heat, and the thermostat should be set at medium. Bacon fat is perfect, as it does not burn and imparts a delicious flavor. Place the cut side of the tomatoes down in the heated fat and cook for 4 minutes; turn carefully with a spatula and cook the other side for 2 or 3 minutes. Remove to a heated platter and keep warm in the oven. When all the tomatoes are fried, add 2 tablespoons of flour to 4 tablespoons of the fat in the pan, stir to blend, and add 3 cups of heated milk. Stir continually until thickened, salt to taste, and pour over the tomatoes. Serve at once. These are especially good for breakfast with scrambled eggs, or as a vegetable with roast beef for dinner.

Helen also gave me her prize recipe, which is for ORANGE-GRAPEFRUIT PIE. Here's how it is prepared, and once you serve it you will probably be known as "Miss Citrus Pie" of your community.

Ingredients:
1 large grapefruit, peeled and cut into small pieces
4 navel oranges, peeled and sectioned
grated rind and juice of 1 lemon
3 tablespoons minute tapioca
⅛ teaspoon salt
1 cup sugar

Mix grapefruit and orange sections with other ingredients and let stand while preparing the pie crust. Pour the mixture into the unbaked crust and cover with a top crust. Bake in a 9-inch pan in a 450°F. oven for 15 minutes, then reduce the heat to 400° for another 20 minutes. I prefer this citrus pie when it is served ice cold.

Ethel Wallace, an artist who lives here in Solebury Township, is a fabulous and extremely creative cook. She has shared several of her inventions with me, and one that I think is especially noteworthy she calls VIENNESE SAUERKRAUT (Choucroute Viennoise). Ethel puts 3 tablespoons of olive oil in a

Dutch oven and sautés 3 cloves of garlic (chopped fine) until slightly brown, removes them from the oil and stirs in 3 tablespoons of tomato paste, adds a #2 can of drained (don't wash it) sauerkraut, stirs to coat with sauce, covers tightly and bakes for 45 minutes in an oven set at 350°F. She served it to 6 with the best roast pork I have ever eaten. This she had done in a very, very slow oven for 4 hours—and I found that even the bones were tender and it was perfectly cooked. There was a flavor which I tried to identify, but it continued to elude me all through the dinner. I naturally asked Ethel what she had used, but she kept changing the subject. Only after we had licked the platter clean and I had even eaten some of the bones did she tell me that she had rubbed the roast with salt, pepper, and *catnip*. All right, don't try it; but you'll be sorry.

Another of Miss Wallace's specialties is LIVER CARMEN. She says the recipe is not original, but with certain touches she really has made it her own. Even people who claim they can't or won't eat liver will relish this, so do try it. Parboil slices of calves' liver slightly. Place in a baking pan and cover with sliced bananas. Season with salt and pepper, and cover with well-buttered bread crumbs. Bake about 15 minutes in a 350°F. oven until brown.

While we are in the banana mood, try this creation of Princess Alexandra Kropotkin's, a dear friend of mine who was an extremely gifted cook, and who prepared this dish while a houseguest of mine here in Bucks County.

Princess Kropotkin's famous cookbook *The Art of Russian Cooking* has recently been republished, and of course you remember her widely read column, "To the Ladies," which appeared for years in *Liberty*. She also wrote frequently about food and its preparation for *Woman's Day*. Knowing my fondness for cooking, Sasha—as she was known to her intimates—often shared with me some of her culinary creations.

For example, try Sasha's HAM-BANANA ROLL-UPS by wrapping thinly sliced smoked ham, spread with a mixture of Dijon mustard and horseradish, around whole, peeled bananas, and securing them with toothpicks or small skewers. Place them in a shallow baking pan, dribble melted butter over them generously, and add some freshly ground black pepper. Bake at 350°F. for about 20 minutes. Serve at once with a pilaf of rice and plenty of Major Grey's Chutney. A green salad, hot rolls and butter. Voilà!

For other examples of Sasha's creative cooking, let me just quote her directly:

"Here is the recipe for the BEET-AND-HORSERADISH ASPIC I promised. As I don't know whether you use canned sliced beets, or fresh, I am just giving amounts. I usually resort to canned sliced beets—less trouble.

2 cups cooked beets, finely chopped or ground
1¾ cups beet juice with 1 tablespoon mild vinegar
*   added*
5 teaspoons prepared (bottled) horseradish

39

> *salt to taste (quite a bit)*
> *2 envelopes plain gelatin*
> *3 tablespoons water*

"Soak the gelatin in water. Drain the beets (if canned); chop or grind very fine. Add the horseradish to the beet juice and vinegar, heat enough to dissolve the gelatin, strain before using.

"Leave the dissolved gelatin to half-set before stirring in the chopped beets (which should be chilled). I like my horseradish strained out of the liquid—some like it left in. Take your choice. Now, the reason for 2 envelopes of gelatin is this: the aspic, whether molded in a loaf form or a ring, should be quite stiff. It goes well with various cold and some hot meats (on shredded lettuce—but no oil, please). Wonderful summer or buffet dish, ring-molded, filled with potato or chicken salad or shrimp or any cold meat.

"And while I'm at it, here is an unusual PORTUGUESE SALAD recipe:

> *2 cucumbers*
> *1 Spanish onion*
> *2 tomatoes*
> *2 apples*
> *2 green peppers*
> *1 tablespoon olive oil*
> *1 tablespoon lemon juice*
> *salt and pepper*
> *1 cup cooked, cut-up chestnuts*

"Peel and cut the cucumbers into very thin slices. Slice the tomatoes and onions. Slice the apples unpeeled but cored. Remove the seeds from the peppers and cut the peppers in thin slices. Combine all the sliced vegetables and fruit, and mix well. Add the lemon juice, olive oil, salt, and pepper. Boil the chestnuts in salted water till tender. Drain and remove from shells. Force the chestnuts through a ricer and sprinkle over the salad. There will be a great plenty for 8 servings.

"And, finally, TORRIJAS DE NATA (Fried Cream), another Portuguese recipe to serve 6:

"Whip 2 lightly beaten egg yolks into 1 cup of heavy cream. Grease a pan well and spread the whipped-cream mixture in it about ½ inch thick. Place over a slow flame and cook very slowly. Allow to cool. Cut in slices. Lift with a spatula. Beat 1 whole egg and brush the slices with the egg. Fry immediately in butter. Serve hot, sprinkled with cinnamon and powdered sugar."

I have eaten all of these at Alexandra's house in New York, and they are absolutely delicious. The Torrijas de Nata is an especially interesting and unusual dessert. Serve it after Paella or Arroz con Pollo to carry out the Latin mood.

Once, at an after-theater supper, Princess Kropotkin served a Welsh Rabbit which has stuck in my memory. She prepared it in a beautiful silver chafing dish and served it on diamond-shaped pieces of toast; but instead of the usual plain toast, hers was spread with Gentleman's Relish. This British

delicacy is, to my knowledge, available only at Fortnum and Mason's in London. It is prepared from a
rare and very old formula, and it is something you
should certainly buy when you go to England. If you
do not plan a trip there in the near future, ask a
friend who is going over to bring you several jars. It
keeps indefinitely and is especially good when mixed
with sweet butter, spread very thinly on fingers of
freshly toasted bread, and passed with the martinis.

Now back to Ethel Wallace, our Bucks County
artist-cook. Ethel frequently serves afternoon tea at
her studio. Her sandwiches of freshly picked watercress are high on my list of favorites, but she also
makes a cake that bears repeating. She calls it
DELICIOUS POTATO CAKE, and she usually serves it on
a day when she also has Constant Comment Tea.

Cream 2 cups of granulated sugar (that's right—2
cups) with ⅔ cup of butter.

Add:
>
> *1 cup hot mashed potatoes*
> *2 squares melted bitter chocolate*
> *½ cup milk*
> *2 cups flour sifted with*
> *2 teaspoons baking powder*

Add:
4 eggs, one at a time, beating after each addition.
Stir in thoroughly:
>
> *1 teaspoon cinnamon*
> *1 teaspoon ground cloves*
> *½ teaspoon grated nutmeg*

Fold in:
   1 cupful chopped walnuts or pecans

Bake in a well-greased spring mold at 325°F. until
the cake springs back when touched gently with a
finger (about 35 minutes). Remove from the pan
when cool. For icing, mix together 1½ cups of granulated sugar, 7 tablespoons of water, and ¾ tablespoon of cider vinegar, and cook until a thread
forms from the spoon. Pour this over the beaten
whites of 2 eggs and beat until peaks form. Flavor
with either pistachio or almond extract. Is that tea
ready yet?

Ethel has recently given me some old "receipts"
from her family's collection, and since they must be
two hundred years old, I am especially intrigued, for
I visualize these things being prepared in the
kitchen of my own house when it was first built. You
may never want to make any of these (except, perhaps, the Dutch Cheese which is excellent as a cocktail snack), but I think it will be amusing to read
about them.

"PEACH LEATHER—Slice some soft peaches, not
otherwise needed for pies or sauce, and mash into a
thin layer on a breakfast plate or pie plate, and put
out in the sun to partially dry. When the juice has
thickened and made the fruit so that it will keep its
shape and can be lifted off the plate, put it into a
stone crock on top of a layer of crushed sugar, and
put more sugar over it. In another day or two, add
another layer, each time putting a generous layer of

sugar between each layer of peach. In the winter, bring out a layer and pass it around to be eaten. The layer of fruit is made quite thin. Before eating, pull it apart in suitable sized pieces.''

''FRIZZLED LIVER—This is a method of curing beef liver to be used in much the same way as dried beef. Cut a liver from a heavy beef, freshly killed, into 2 or 3 pieces, place in a vessel large enough to hold it conveniently, and cover with a brine made of water in which has been dissolved enough common salt to float an egg. Add a pinch of salt petre to the brine. Allow the liver to remain in the brine for about 2 weeks, then take it out and hang by a string to the kitchen ceiling until it dries, so that there is no danger of mold. This process is best accomplished during the winter months. When it is dried, wrap securely in newspaper and hang in cellar way or closet. Thinly sliced and frizzled in butter with cream added, this is a most delicious and tasty dish. A favorite First-day morning dish, it has a delicate, unusual flavor; and there is never such an abundance that the family grows tired of it.''

''DUTCH CHEESE—To some rich cottage cheese, add enough finely cut sage leaves or rubbed dry ones to give the mass a pleasant flavor. Make this into balls, and put away on the cellar shelf until it ripens or ages about a week. By this time a skin will form on the outside, and when this is cut off 'Dutch Cheese' is left. Delicious served with dessert, especially if the dessert is a juicy rhubarb, cherry, or peach pie.''

44

We must admit that the ladies who kept hearth and home two hundred years ago were ingenious. They had to be! They had never heard of icy Frigidaires, or Cold Spot Freezers. I sometimes wish we hadn't either, for no one in America seems to want to cook. I do not understand why, but I strongly suspect that television has had some influence on our eating habits. Too many families now choose to gather in front of the box for their evening meal. Mama, not to be denied her share of the newest All-American pastime, rushes about in the kitchen warming up TV dinners. Someone I know recently remarked that he had eaten so many of these that every time he sees a piece of foil he gets hungry. What a sad, albeit illuminating, commentary on our new way of life.

British-born Rosemary White migrated to Bucks County by way of Virginia. She has a regal air about her, so it is difficult to picture her in the kitchen, but I have seen her there and she can cook most expertly when the mood is on her.

Rosemary was taught how to prepare TUTTI-FRUTTI by her mother-in-law's Virginia cook. However, Rosemary has improved the original by adding a touch of her own, and quite a touch it is. She uses 180-proof grain alcohol instead of the 86-proof brandy they use in Virginia.

I have gone her one better and added Cherry Heering along with the alcohol. One starts Tutti-Frutti in the spring, with pineapples peeled and cut up into 1-inch cubes. For each cup of fruit you add 1 cup of sugar. This requires a stone crock with a tight-fitting lid, and you add strawberries, raspberries, blackberries (not too many), seedless grapes, wild cherries (pitted or not as you prefer), peaches, and other fruits as they come into season, always adding the same amount of sugar as fruit. For a 3-gallon crock of fruit, I use a pint of 180-proof alcohol and a pint of Cherry Heering. Add more if you like. Live dangerously! Serve at Thanksgiving and Christmas spooned over vanilla ice cream. Serve Hershey's Chocolate Sauce, instead, to the one who is driving home.

One evening Rosemary had 8 for dinner, and she was the most relaxed hostess-cook I ever saw. She served LEG OF LAMB as the main course. Absolutely mouth-watering, and I all but beat her until she told me the secret. She made the usual slits with a knife and inserted thin slices of garlic. But she also made deeper and wider slits in which she put anchovy filets; then the roast was placed in a hot oven after being well seasoned with cracked black peppercorns. After 15 minutes, the fat was poured off, 2 cans of beef consommé were heated and poured into the roasting pan, the oven was turned back to 300°, and with each round of martinis the roast was basted with a cocktail glass of gin. Rosemary serves her lamb just slightly pink near the bone. If you like yours any other way, by all means use a meat thermometer. I can't tell you how long to cook a roast. I do mine by ear, and so does Rosemary.

With the lamb, Rosemary served LEEKS MORNAY.

She trimmed 10 large leeks and washed them, then cut off all but about an inch of green. They were quartered and gently boiled in salted water for 10 minutes, then drained and placed in a shallow casserole. She made a cream sauce using 2 tablespoons of butter, 1 tablespoon of flour, 1 cup of milk, and a cupful of the water in which the leeks had been boiled. When it was thickened she added a cup of shredded Swiss cheese, a dash of cayenne and another of nutmeg. Then ½ jigger of brandy was stirred in after the sauce was removed from the stove. It was poured over the leeks, then a generous dribble of melted butter and a handful of shredded cheese were sprinkled over the top. Finally, paprika, and into a hot oven until the cheese melted and the sauce bubbled. Next time I hope she will make enough so the guests can have "thirds."

Another part-time New Yorker—Hope Hendler, the hat designer and Francophile supreme—is also a neighbor in Bucks County. She too lives in a fabulous old stone house, but her place is a genuine farm, which supplies most of the fresh vegetables used by Horn and Hardart's Philadelphia restaurants. Hope not only designs very chic millinery and does an occasional decorating job for affluent friends, but she has also found time to become a French cook par excellence. At the drop of one of her chapeaux she can sail into la cuisine and emerge an hour later bearing Quiche Lorraine, a salad beyond description, and a Gâteau Chocolat. She once told me that she had gone through an entire inheritance from an

47

obscure cousin at Colette's Pâtisserie on Third Avenue in New York. She decided it would be less expensive and more fun to do her own Quiche and Gâteau. It may not be cheaper—especially the way Hope does it—but it is certainly a lot more exciting if you are fortunate enough to be her guest.

GÂTEAU CHOCOLAT—Melt ¼ pound of bitter chocolate, and mix with 3 ounces of softened butter, ¼ pound of sugar, a pinch of salt, 2 tablespoons of flour, and 4 beaten egg yolks. Fold in the remaining egg whites, stiffly beaten. Bake in a bread-loaf pan, well greased with sweet butter, in a 350°F. oven for 35 minutes.

Directly across Fleecydale Road from me is The Vintage. It is the residence of Mr. and Mrs. John Vint, and no one could ever hope to have more thoughtful, kind, and considerate neighbors. They bought their house (stone, naturally) about eight years ago, and have had many hilarious experiences (to say nothing of considerable expense) restoring it. When I was commuting to New York, Nan Vint looked after my house as well as her own. She watered my plants and kept her eye on everything. What a joy it was to arrive here from New York on a wintry Friday night to find the lights on, the heat turned up, and a fresh pie or cake covered with a tea towel on the kitchen table.

Nan once lent me an ancient cookbook which had belonged to her grandmother. It was so well thumbed it was literally falling apart. She told me how much it meant to her, not only for sentimental reasons, but because it was the most useful cookbook she had ever owned.

It was near Christmas, and I had wracked my brain to think of a proper gift for the Vints, as a proper gesture of gratitude. The ancient cookbook gave me the answer. I took it into town and found a bookbinder who, though swamped with holiday orders, promised to have it re-bound by December 24. He did—and wish I could recapture here for you the look on Nan's face when she opened her "gift."

Here, instead, are four recipes from the old cookbook. Nan and I have experimented and brought them up to date. They are real country fare, and what can be better?

FASTNACHTS (Raised Doughnuts)

Sponge:

> *1 cake yeast*
> *2 cups lukewarm water*
> *4 scant cups sifted flour*
> *1 teaspoon sugar*

At night break and soak yeast in lukewarm water for 20 minutes. Mix with flour to a thick batter. Cover, let rise in warm place overnight until doubled.

Dough:

> *½ cup shortening*
> *⅜ cup sugar*
> *1½ teaspoons salt*
> *2 eggs*

49

> *½ teaspoon ground nutmeg (optional)*
> *5 cups or more of flour*

In morning cream together shortening, sugar, and salt. Add this to the risen sponge, with the beaten eggs and spice. Stir in as much flour as mixture will take up readily, making a rather soft dough. Mix well. Let rise until doubled in bulk. If desired, stir down and let rise again until nearly doubled, as this second rise creates a slightly finer texture. Turn onto floured board, pat or roll ⅓-inch thick, and cut with doughnut cutter. Fry in deep hot fat about 375°F. Makes 2 dozen doughnuts.

OLD-FASHIONED GINGER COOKIES

Mix together thoroughly:
> *⅓ cup soft shortening*
> *1 cup brown sugar*
> *1½ cups black molasses*

Stir in ½ cup cold water
Sift together & stir in:
> *6 cups sifted flour*
> *1 teaspoon salt*
> *1 teaspoon allspice*
> *1 teaspoon ginger*
> *1 teaspoon cloves*
> *1 teaspoon cinnamon*

Stir in 2 teaspoons soda dissolved in 3 tablespoons cold water.

Chill dough, then roll out ½-inch thick and cut with 2½-inch round cutter. Place far apart on greased baking sheet. Bake until, when touched lightly with finger, no imprint remains. Temperature: 350°F. (moderate oven). Time: 15 to 18 minutes. Amount: About 2⅔ dozen.

Can also be iced with following: Blend together 1 cup sifted 10X sugar, ¼ teaspoon salt, and ½ teaspoon vanilla with enough water or milk to make easy to spread (about 1½ tablespoons).

World's Best Biscuits—Pennsylvania Dutch

In Nan Vint's words: "Sift 6 cups of flour, 1 teaspoon of salt and 4 teaspoons of baking powder. Gradually add 2 cups of sour cream, working as little as possible. Turn out on floured board and press out with hands. Do not roll. Cut with biscuit cutter and bake in hot oven (400°F.) for about 10 minutes. This makes about 3 dozen biscuits. This is the original recipe. I usually make half the quantity at a time as it is easier to handle. I use either Gold Medal flour or Hecker's (if I can get it). I use *light* sour cream. This is the usual kind—but some places have a heavy kind. I do *not* use a biscuit cutter, but pinch off bits and hand-shape them, the way MacPherson ('The Mystery Chef') taught me. In my oven 400° is quite hot—and I find another 5 to 10 minutes in a slower oven, after the first 10 at 400°, is needed. As you know, no two ovens are alike."

To make Hootsla, or Egg Bread, get a half-loaf of day-old bread (better yet, 2-day-old cracked-wheat bread), ½ cup of butter, 3 eggs, beaten till very light, ½ cup of milk, some salt and pepper. Cut the bread into cubes, and brown them in butter or bacon fat. Add the eggs, mixed with milk, salt and pepper (go slow on salt.) Pour over the bread, fry 2 minutes, or longer as desired. I cut up the "bread omelette" in the pan as it fries, and serve it with crisp bacon or frizzled ham. Ideal for 2.

A dessert that my Bucks County guests never fail to rave about, and which at the same time is quite simple to prepare, is my own version of Crème Brûlée. I call it COFFEE CUSTARD BRULÉE, and here is how it is done:

Blend together ½ cup of sugar, a pinch of salt, and a tablespoon of instant coffee; break 4 eggs into a bowl and stir gently until blended with the sugar mixture; add 1 pint of light cream, 1 pint of milk, and ½ cup of rum. Pour into a shallow casserole, and set in a pan of water. Bake at 300°F. until the custard is set (a knife inserted in center will come out clean). Chill in refrigerator. When cold, cover the top with ¼ inch of light-brown sugar. (I sift it with a flour sifter over the top.) Place under the broiler until the sugar melts. Refrigerate until ready to serve (or for at least 3 hours.) This makes 8 servings.

Another dessert that seems to please my guests is individual ORANGE ALASKAS.

Select the largest available oranges, cut off the tops (about ¼ of the way down), and carefully scoop out the juice and pulp from the remaining ¾ section. Fill the shells with a well-frozen Italian orange water ice or orange sherbet.

Prepare the meringue in advance, using the white of an egg for each orange. Beat the egg whites, to which you add a pinch of cream of tartar for each, until very stiff but not dry. Carefully fold in 1 teaspoon of Grand Marnier for each egg white.

Cover the orange ice completely, building the meringue into a cone. Sprinkle with grated orange peel, and set the oranges into a muffin pan to hold them in position. (I always put chopped ice in the bottom of each pan.) Bake in a quick oven until the meringue is browned, and serve at once.

My favorite dessert was served at the Sheraton-East Hotel. It is POT DE CRÈME AU CHOCOLAT, for which Chef Henri Heller has given me his recipe.

For 12 servings: Mix 6 ounces of sugar, 10 egg yolks, ½ pint of light cream, and 2 teaspoons of vanilla in a bowl. Heat another ¾ pint of light cream with 6 ounces of shaved Menier chocolate until the chocolate is melted, and add to the first mixture. Strain into 12 individual pots. Place them in a pan of water and put into a 300°F. oven for about 30 minutes—until set. Cool and refrigerate.

I wonder if Chef Heller has ever served this delectable concoction to the President and Lady Bird? Henri is now Chef de Cuisine at the White House. He was engaged for his present position as a result of having served the President and First Lady when they frequently stayed at the Sheraton-East Hotel as Senator and Mrs. Johnson. I envy the visiting dignitaries who are dining so well under the aegis of this gifted man.

The sister of my good friend Marguerite Jordan lives in Alabama, and every year at Christmas she sends Marguerite a WHITE FRUITCAKE which she makes in October. I do not care for fruitcake as a rule, but this is something very special indeed, and I look forward to sharing this delightful confection each year. This has always been a closely guarded family secret, but with a little wheeler-dealing on my part I am now prepared to expose this exquisite delight to the world.

Bake it in fairly small pans, and give it to special friends as the most thoughtful gift they are likely to receive. You will require the following ingredients:

1 pound butter
1 pound sugar
1 dozen eggs
1 pound flour
1 teaspoon baking powder
1 pound crystallized cherries
1 pound crystallized pineapple
2 pounds white raisins
½ pound citron
½ pound orange peel
¼ pound lemon peel
cognac
1 grated nutmeg
2 teaspoons lemon extract
2 teaspoons grated lemon peel
2 pounds chopped nuts: brazil (with brown hulls removed), pistachio, blanched almonds

Bucks County

Cream the butter and sugar, separate the eggs, and stir in the yolks one at a time, add flour (already sifted with baking powder) a cupful at a time, and blend thoroughly.

Add all the fruit, which has been soaked in cognac overnight. Don't overdo the brandy—just enough to saturate the fruit. Stir in the nutmeg, lemon extract, and lemon peel. Then the chopped nutmeats.

Lastly beat the 12 egg whites, plus 1 extra egg white (for good luck), until stiff, and fold them gently into the cake mixture. Makes 4 8 × 8-inch cakes.

Bake at 250°F. about 3½ hours. Cool in the pans. Wrap each cake in heavy aluminum foil, or store in individual tin boxes with tight-fitting covers. Once a week, remove the cover and douse each cake with brandy. Eventually, ice with boiled icing, and decorate with almonds, cherries, and candied violets.

While still in this Southern frame of mind, let's make a PECAN PIE. Into a rich-pastry, unbaked pie shell pour the following mixture which you have beaten at medium speed in your electric beater:

> *4 eggs*
> *1½ cups light-brown sugar*
> *1 cup white corn syrup*
> *1 stick whipped butter, or oleomargarine*
> *1 teaspoon vanilla extract*

Cover with ½ pound of pecan halves. Place in a 400°F. oven for 10 minutes. Reduce heat to 350° and bake another 30 minutes. Serve with vanilla ice cream, or whipped cream. Tomorrow you can start the Metrecal.

Today is a beautiful October day. I am sitting on the terrace and the birds are busy in the barberry bushes. It is 80°. Nan Vint has just come over and brought another of her marvelous family recipes; one her mother did each year. This recipe of her grandmother's, for STRAWBERRY PRESERVES, is well worth keeping in mind for the time when spring returns.

Select firm, ripe berries, and hull and wash them in cold water after a quick blanching in hot water. Using a large-bottomed kettle, alternate the berries with sprinklings of sugar in layers. Let stand for 15 minutes to draw out the juice, and then simmer for 5 minutes. Skim well, then lift out the berries, draining them thoroughly of all syrup, and arrange in single layers on platters or plates. Boil the syrup down thick, 220° F. on a candy thermometer, or until the syrup threads slightly. Pour this thick syrup—while hot—over the berries.

When sufficiently cool, place by a sunny window, or cover with a sheet of glass or cheesecloth and place in direct sunlight for ten or twelve hours. If the sun is not bright and steady, allow the platters to remain for 3 or 4 days, or until the syrup is nearly jellied; then fill hot, sterile jars to ½ inch from the top. Adjust the rubbers, partially seal the covers, and sterilize in boiling water 10 minutes or in a 250°F. oven 20 minutes. Seal and cool.

The Women's Fellowship of Carversville—my

adopted village—published a cookbook in 1956, and the diversity shows how fully the neighborhood ladies, as well as some of the men, gave their favorite recipes. For example, Mrs. D. Deens's OLD-TIME SHOO-FLY PIE:

After having lined the pie tins with dough, take 1½ cups of boiling water, pour over 1 teaspoon of baking soda, and stir into 1 cup of dark molasses. Pour the liquid mixture into the crust, making it about ½ full. Then make crumbs by mixing together the following:

4 cups flour
2 cups brown sugar
1 cup butter
2 scant tablespoons cinnamon, or to suit taste

Sprinkle the crumbs into the liquid. Bake in a moderate oven, as for a loaf cake. This makes 2 delicious Shoo-Fly pies. (Do not bake the crust separately—bake the whole pie together.)

The BLACK-WALNUT LOAF CAKE omits the name of the contributor, but I can assure all black-walnut lovers that this is for them.

Cream:
½ cup butter
1 cup plus 2 tablespoons sugar
2 unbeaten eggs
1 teaspoon vanilla
1 teaspoon orange juice

Mix together:

>   *2 cups cake flour*
>   *2½ teaspoons baking powder*
>   *¾ teaspoon salt*

Add to first mixture with ¾ cup milk. Last, add ¾ cup broken black-walnuts. Bake 1 hour and 10 minutes. Frost with an orange butter frosting.

Odessa Wintriss gives us a SAUERBRATEN that is especially good. I serve it with noodles covered with buttered bread crumbs, as I long ago gave up trying to make potato dumplings. You may agree that this is the best sauerbraten recipe you have ever tried.

For 8 to 10 servings:

>   *3 to 4 pounds chuck, rump, or shoulder beef*
>   *2 teaspoons salt*
>   *½ teaspoon pepper*
>   *2 cups vinegar*
>   *6 whole cloves*
>   *2 cups water*
>   *3 onions, sliced*
>   *2 bay leaves*
>   *1 teaspoon peppercorns*

If the beef is very dry, lard it with thin strips of fat pork or bacon. Rub salt and pepper into the meat and place it in a large bowl. Heat the rest of ingredients together, but do not boil, and pour while hot over the meat to more than half cover. Keep in a tightly covered bowl 4 or 5 days in the refrigerator, turning the meat daily. When ready to cook, drain and save the liquid. Brown the beef on all sides in hot fat in a Dutch oven or heavy kettle.

Add 2 cups of the marinade and some freshly sliced onions. If the vinegar is too sour, dilute it with water. Cover tightly and cook over low heat 2 or 3 hours, or until the beef is very tender. Remove the beef. Strain the liquid and thicken it with browned flour or a few finely crumbled ginger snaps.

Mrs. Wintriss recently made a very special loaf of bread which was served at the Sunday Communion service at the local church. This bread was indeed a labor of love, for Mrs. Wintriss had grown the wheat, ground it into flour, and then used a very old "receipt" in the preparation. You see, these Bucks County folk are a rare breed.

The other evening I was served an unusual COMBINATION CHRISTMAS PIE that turned out to be not only delicious but quite logical in concept. Hal Helsel, who lives in Lumberville, noted that during the holiday season many people asked for servings of both pumpkin and mincemeat pie when available, and so he decided to combine both in the same pie. Terrific! Don't mix them, however, but put a generous layer of mincemeat into an unbaked pie shell, then over it put pumpkin-pie mix, using a little less milk than usual. Place in a hot oven (425°F.) for 10 minutes, then reduce heat to 350° for about 30 minutes. Cut 8 wedges of sharp cheddar cheese—take the pie out of the oven and lay the pieces of cheese on top—return to the oven for about 10 minutes, or until the cheese has melted slightly. Serve warm.

Recently when guests were coming I made GAME

Game Hens in Sauce / Rice

HENS IN SAUCE. I roasted Rock Cornish Game Hens after seasoning them well with salt, pepper, and rosemary. I then mixed 1 cup of honey with 1 cup of vinegar, heated it, and used the mixture to baste the hens every 10 minutes while they were roasting.

There was no wild rice in the pantry, so I used some quick-cooking rice, trying a trick I had learned from my friend Maria Towne. (Maria is of Greek descent, but she is married to an Italian, spends three months each year in Italy, and is a true Italophile to the *nth* degree.) Maria sautés sliced mushrooms and strips of green pepper in butter with a little garlic-flavored olive oil for 5 minutes. Then she adds a few wedges of fresh tomato (I use yellow ones when available.) Cook another 5 minutes and stir into the hot rice. MARIA'S RICE is a perfect complement to chicken or veal.

Speaking of chicken and veal, here are two good ways to fix them. For the veal, have the butcher prepare cutlets from the veal leg and flatten them with the side of the cleaver. Place them in a shallow pan, cover with light cream, and allow to marinate at room temperature for 2 or 3 hours. Remove from cream—do not dry—but dip into flour that has been seasoned with salt and cracked black pepper. Sauté the cutlets in butter and remove to a heated platter. To the pan add the remainder of the cream in which you soaked the veal, mixed with 2 beaten egg yolks, and stir continually over a hot flame until slightly thickened. Add ½ cup of chopped Italian parsley, and pour over the cutlets. VITELLO ECCELLENTE!

And now the chicken, which I call POLLO ALLA

60

Broc. Partly bone-out breasts of chicken (plan ½ for each serving) and sauté them in butter until well browned. Remove and place in a casserole which has a lid. Stir 1 envelope of Knorr Cream-of-Leek Soup Mix into the butter in the pan. To this add 1 cup of sherry, 1 cup of hot water, and 1 cup of light cream. Stir over a low flame until thickened. Pour over the chicken, put on the cover, and bake 25 minutes in an oven set at 350°F. A slice of truffle on each serving adds a touch of glamour, but you can substitute chopped ripe olives for effect as well as for a pleasant change from the inevitable parsley.

Editor, men's fashion authority, lecturer, writer, Robert L. Green is a most successful and urbane young gentleman who last year bought an exceptionally beautiful old stone house here in Bucks County. It is situated high on a hill overlooking the valley, and the view is spectacular. Robert is here as a rule from Thursday until Sunday night. The rest of the week—when he is not in London, or Beverly Hills, or Aswan, or Rome—he is in New York, where he has a handsome town house.

Here in the country Robert enjoys most of all getting into the kitchen; and he thinks nothing of inviting thirty or forty guests for Sunday luncheon. He makes so many unusual and extremely interesting creations that it is difficult to pick out one or two to include here. In summer he features delicious aspics and mousses which are prepared in his collection of antique molds. He lifts them out of the usual by secret touches of fresh herbs and the deft use of wines. He is not an outdoor-barbecue fanatic, and

61

what a relief. Few people have his food-imagination, or the willingness to devote time to the preparation of fine victuals.

One of Robert's favorite dishes is SHRIMP MOUSSE. Prepare 2 packages of celery-flavored gelatin, using half the amount of water suggested. Add ½ cup of dry sherry and allow to cool. Meanwhile, beat 4 egg whites until very stiff, and fold in 1 cup of sour cream and a tablespoonful of fresh tarragon leaves. Combine the gelatin, which is by now partly set, with the second mixture; fold in 3 cups of peeled and de-veined shrimp cut into small pieces. Rinse your favorite mold with cold water and pour in the mousse. Leave in the refrigerator at least four hours (overnight is better).

Unmold on a bed of watercress, and "ice" with a thin cover of mayonnaise. Garnish with small Danish shrimp arranged in a pattern. The mayonnaise will hold them in place. This makes 8 generous servings.

Serve with a RUSSIAN VEGETABLE SALAD made with cold cooked peas, julienne carrots (cooked), canned mushroom caps and tiny pearl onions. The dressing should be mayonnaise thinned with tarragon vinegar and seasoned with garlic powder and a dash of cayenne. Mix carefully to avoid mashing the vegetables.

A good friend, Katy Houghton, who owns an outstanding antique shop here in the county, recently invited me to dinner at her lovely home and she served HAM AND SAUTÉED OYSTERS, an old Pennsylvania Dutch creation which makes me even more appreciative than ever of their food sense.

First, bake a ham. One of those from the Bemis Market is absolutely perfect. (See Index.)

For each guest plan to use 6 large frying oysters. Use a heavy skillet and in it put ¼ pound of sweet butter. Heat over a hot flame until the butter is very well browned—in fact, slightly burned (beurre noir). Then lower the heat and sauté 3 or 4 oysters at a time. Do not try to cook too many at once as they should be done quickly, turned once, and then placed in a double-boiler and sprinkled with dry sherry. They can be prepared well before dinner, so you will be able to relax with the guests during cocktails.

To serve, slice the ham rather thin, and place the oysters on each slice together with some of the juices which have accumulated. Add to the beurre noir 2 tablespoons of flour and stir to blend, then add 1 cup of hot water and ½ cup of sherry. Cook until thickened and pour over the oysters.

Ruth and Wilbur Manning are a delightful couple who are more or less newcomers to Bucks County. They have a charming house in Doylestown, where they entertain in a totally relaxed and ingratiating manner. Ruth is a wonderful cook, kind enough to part with her Aunt Lou's recipe for BLUEBERRY PUDDING.

Combine:
1 cup granulated sugar
1½ cups blueberries (or any other fruit or berry
       preferred by your family)
1 cup boiling water

Cook this for 5 minutes while you prepare the batter.

Stir together:
>1½ *cups flour*
>½ *cup sugar*
>1 *cup milk*
>1 *egg*
>4 *tablespoons melted butter*
>1 *teaspoon baking powder*
>1 *teaspoon vanilla*

Place in a well-greased 1½-quart casserole. Pour the fruit over the batter and bake in a 350°F. oven for 35 minutes. The batter comes up to the top, while the delicious fruit sauce stays at the bottom. Serve warm with whipped cream or ice cream to 6 or 8 eager guests.

Ruth makes the best CHRISTMAS COOKIES I have ever tasted, and being an excellent amateur painter she decorates them beautifully, actually "painting" each cookie with various colored sugar icings.

To make the cookies you will need:
>1 *cup granulated sugar*
>½ *pound butter*
>2 *whole eggs*
>1 *teaspoon baking soda*
>1 *teaspoon cream of tartar*
>2 *tablespoons sweet cream*
>1 *teaspoon vanilla*
>4 *cups sifted flour*

Cream the sugar with the butter, add the eggs, and beat well. Add the sweet cream and vanilla. Add 1 cup of flour sifted with the cream of tartar and baking soda. Then add one at a time 3 more cups of sifted flour. Place dough in refrigerator for an hour, then roll out a little at a time, very thin, and cut into various shapes. Bake in a 400°F. oven. This makes about 6 to 8 dozen, depending on the size of cookie-cutter used.

Bradley Bransford has an unusual old stone house which was once an early settler's hunting lodge, and since Brad is a transplanted Texan he has taught later settlers the wonders of CHILI. I have inveigled the recipe from him.

You will require:
4 pounds lean beef (cut into small cubes and dusted
with flour)
½ cup olive oil
3 slivered garlic cloves
6 onions, chopped
1 large can Italian peeled tomatoes
3 tablespoons chili powder
salt to taste
1 small can green chili peppers
1 teaspoon cumin

Sauté the meat in a heavy skillet in the olive oil with the garlic cloves. Do it a little at a time so it will brown well, and then place the meat in a large pot, adding the onions, the can of tomatoes, and the 3 tablespoons of really good (and hot) chili powder.

Salt to taste. Cover and cook over a low flame for about 2 hours, or until the meat is tender. Do not overcook it. Now add the green chili peppers and cumin. The chili can be served as is with red kidney beans—well seasoned with sautéed green peppers and oregano—and freshly steamed rice. However, I prefer to add 3 cans of red kidney beans to the meat, heat well, and serve in bowls with a spoonful of rice on top. There will be plenty for 8 persons. Whatever your preference, I assure you this is the native Texans' Chili, with the knowledgeable approval of my good friends Ann and Bernard Sakowitz of Houston.

A well-chilled avocado-and-grapefruit salad served on a bed of chicory is a good accompaniment. It soothes the taste buds. If you must serve bread make it corn bread, and serve it warm with plenty of sweet butter.

By now I am sure you realize that Bucks County is uniquely cosmopolitan and heterogeneous. Those of us who have moved here have brought with us the know-how of food preparation from various parts of America and abroad, and, being adaptable folk, soon made the Pennsylvania-type foods a part of our cuisine.

One notable feature of Bucks County is its seemingly endless fields of corn. Country Gentleman and Golden Bantam corn are grown on every plot of available farmland in the county. City dwellers coming to the country during corn season are astounded at the difference between the corn they buy in even the very best city markets and that which they eat down here. The secret is not so much the corn itself as the fact that once the luscious ears are pulled from the stalks, they are not ever refrigerated, but husked and cooked immediately while the milk is at its peak. Friends who never otherwise eat corn come to Bucks County and indulge in four or five ears unashamedly.

The native Americans—now called Indians—were enjoying maize at least a thousand years before Amerigo Vespucci. They had developed methods of growing and using the golden harvest which makes me wonder if this is not what inspired Pizzaro to come to these shores in search of the gold he had dreamed grew on trees.

Maybe the Indians didn't teach the first settlers to make clam chowder, but they did them an even greater favor by introducing them to their own staple food, which is now one of America's and the world's major crops.

Some of the very earliest visitors to the Colonies returned to England to write glowingly of the corn, giving full credit to the Indians for teaching the settlers how to raise and use this fascinating food. It is recorded history that on more than one occasion the corn crop saved our forebears from starvation.

The by-products we now take for granted run from cornflakes to corn-oil margarine. How could we make pecan pie without corn syrup? Or thicken puddings without cornstarch? Wouldn't you dislike doing forever without corn "likker"? And if you are a Southerner, can you imagine your breakfast eggs served up plain without hominy grits?

The Pennsylvania Dutch have made great use of corn in their "plain food," their pancakes made with buckwheat flour, cornmeal, and a touch of molasses being country fare at its very best. Their simple meal of fried cornmeal mush and homemade sausage, served with dried apples which they soak in water before frying, is one of the reasons they have remained a healthy people almost immune to the aches and pains of "outsiders."

My Great Aunt Nell, who passed away at the age of ninety-odd more from ennui than anything else, once told me that the only reason she had remained healthy all her life was due to the big bowl of cornmeal mush she had eaten every morning until she was twenty years old. She did not stop eating it then, but merely had it less frequently, always with maple syrup and warm milk poured over it.

One fall some friends and I had spent a day trimming brush, and had made a huge fire to burn the gathered branches. We were standing near the fire admiring our work and enjoying a pitcher of martinis when someone suggested we pick some corn, which was right then at its peak, and roast it in the ashes of our fire.

This turned out to be one of the unforgettable experiences of my life. First we picked four ears of corn each and put it unhusked into the brook to dampen thoroughly. While we started the charcoal in three habachis, someone went to the house to get thick lamb chops from the refrigerator. Another ambitious guest picked a salad bowl full of Swiss chard, and off she went to the kitchen to prepare her special salad.

Too many cooks do not always spoil the broth, and this meal was proof positive. While one cook tended the lamb chops sizzling on the grills, another fished the corn out of the brook and raked it into the glowing coals of the bonfire, where it stayed for fifteen minutes. By now the hot Pennsylvania-Dutch dressing was ready to pour over and wilt the Swiss chard, and six very contented (all's-right-with-the-world contentment) people sat around the embers of the fire and ate far into the gathering twilight.

I once knew a girl who looked exactly like Dolores del Rio, and everyone treated her as though she really were the famed beauty. She was so pampered that when she married she knew nothing about even the rudiments of cooking. Her husband, who—believe it or not—looked like Rudolph Valentino, mentioned one day that corn on the cob was his most favorite food.

Off went the bride to buy a dozen ears of corn which she brought home and laboriously husked. She put them into the largest kettle possible, filled it to the brim with cold water, and at 9:00 a.m. put it on to cook. At 5:30 p.m. it was still boiling rapidly and the bride was on the verge of tears. She was sure it would never be done in time for dinner. When the Sheik of Araby arrived, ravenously hungry and eager, she explained as best she could why his favorite dish was not ready. "I have boiled it all day, and I still can't stick a fork in the cobs."

She now knows—and still looks like Miss del Rio—that you put a small amount of water with a spoonful of sugar into a pot, put in the corn when the water is boiling, cover and steam for no more than five minutes. Remove from heat and serve immediately with lots of butter. Let the guests salt to their taste.

The John F. Cope Company, Inc., of Manheim, Lancaster County, Pennsylvania, specializes in Pennsylvania-Dutch products, featuring Dried Sweet Corn which I recommend most heartily. You can stew it, bake it, pressure-cook it, fritter it, or make it into a wonderful corn soup.

Since it is dried you must soak it, and while they suggest using boiling water, I use hot milk. After it has soaked for an hour or more, you may proceed as with canned corn.

I make a CREAM-OF-CORN SOUP, using a thin cream sauce flavored with onion and crumbled crisp bacon to which I add one cup of corn for each quart of soup. Use popcorn instead of croutons as a garnish.

For a hearty breakfast, make CORN GRIDDLE CAKES, using a batter of prepared corn-muffin mix, adding an extra egg and an extra cup of evaporated milk with 1 tablespoon of vinegar and ½ teaspoon of baking soda stirred into it, plus a cup of corn, either canned cream-style or reconstituted dried. Drop the batter by spoonfuls onto a well-greased pancake griddle. Turn once, and serve immediately with butter and maple syrup. Fried country ham or sausage makes this a meal to warm the cockles on the snowiest day in January.

My stepmother, Birdena, makes the world's best JOHNNY CAKE, and here is her recipe:

1 cup yellow cornmeal
1 cup white flour
2 tablespoons sugar
½ teaspoon salt
4 teaspoons baking powder
1 whole egg
1 cup milk
4 tablespoons melted butter

Stir all together, and bake in a hot oven (425°F.) in a well-greased square pan for about 20 minutes.

Serve it cut into squares with lots of butter, and it goes with almost any meal. Or cut it into squares and top it with creamed chicken and diced ham as a shortcake for the main course of a luncheon. Red currant jelly is a perfect accompaniment.

SUCCOTASH (from the Indian word "Misickquatash") was introduced to the colonists in Virginia by the aborigines. The canned or frozen varieties will do in a pinch, but once you make it with corn freshly cut from the cob and cooked in milk (for no more than 10 minutes), to which you add freshly hulled lima beans which have been quickly boiled in a minimum of water and plenty of butter until barely tender, then you will understand why John Smith married Pocahontas. She was the best Misickquatash maker in all of "ole Virginny."

Down South the famous SPOONBREAD is on every good cook's list. My friend Marguerite Jordan, who was born in the Tidewater section of Virginia, taught me how to make it. For this you must have water-ground cornmeal, the best of which, strangely enough, comes from Virginia. Most good markets stock it so it should present no problem. For 1 cup of cornmeal use 4 cups of whole milk. Heat the milk to boiling, and stir in the cornmeal, cooking (better use a double-boiler) until slightly thickened. Remove from the fire and add 3 tablespoons of butter and 1½ teaspoons of salt. Beat the yolks of 5 eggs and add, stirring well. Have ready the whites of 6 eggs which you have beaten very stiff and to which you have added 1 teaspoon of baking powder. Fold the cornmeal mixture into the egg whites very gently. Pour into a well-buttered 2-quart baking dish. Bake in a 400°F. oven about 45 minutes. Be sure the guests are at the table, and serve at once with plenty of butter. This will serve 3 to 4. For 6 or 8 hearty eaters I double the recipe, baking half for 30 minutes, then putting the other half in the oven so it comes out when the first batch is eaten. It is really a soufflé the way Marguerite does it.

The PENNSYLVANIA-DUTCH CORN PUDDING is made by cutting the corn from 8 large ears, and scraping the ears with a knife to remove all the milk. Separate 4 eggs and beat the yolks and whites separately. First add the yolks to the corn, then ½ cup of cream, 1 teaspoon of salt, and ½ teaspoon of pepper (a tablespoonful of sugar is good also). Carefully fold the corn mixture into the beaten whites and pour into a 1-quart casserole. Bake in a pan of hot water at 350°F. for ½ hour. This makes a quart of corn custard deluxe the way the "plain people" do it.

Many varieties of CORN RELISH are sold commercially, but the kind you make at home is so easy to do and so superior you really should try it.

You will need the following ingredients to make 6 pints:

> *24 ears of spanking fresh corn*
> *6 green peppers*
> *6 red peppers*
> *6 large Bermuda onions*
> *4 cups sugar*
> *5 cups vinegar*
> *2 tablespoons each of:*
>   *salt*
>   *celery seed*
>   *dry mustard*
>   *turmeric*
> *1 cup water*

Some people add a head of cabbage chopped, but I do not. Suit yourself.

Cut the corn off the cobs; chop the peppers (do not grind them) and the onions. Put all the ingredients into a large kettle and boil for 30 minutes, stirring occasionally. Seal in scalded jars while hot.

Serve it with hamburgers, roast beef, or what-have-you. Ralph Strain, the well-known café-society

pianist, has it for breakfast on hot buttered toast.
The last time he visited here he took home six jars.
There are those who eat cornflakes. Ralph eats Corn
Relish. (I even know a girl who likes roast-pork
gravy on apple pie. She is not, however, a member of
La Société de Tastevin.)

Ethel Wallace's delicious GREEN CORN CAKES are
made by grating 6 large ears of corn and adding 2
well-beaten egg yolks, a pinch of salt, and a sprinkle
of brown sugar. No milk, cream, or flour in these.
Heat the griddle and put on it a lump of butter half
the size of an egg. Then drop the mixture by table-
spoonfuls onto the griddle, fry until a light brown,
turn with a spatula and cook thoroughly. This makes
about 2 dozen cakes.

An unusual and very good luncheon dish is CORN
RABBIT, prepared with 2 cups of corn freshly cut
from the cobs and sautéed in a generous amount of
butter in a pan with a tight-fitting lid. Cook briskly
for about 5 minutes, then stir in three cupfuls of
your favorite Welsh Rabbit and add one cup of
diced, cooked ham. Serve from a chafing dish on
halves of toasted English Muffins. You will please 6
people.

POPCORN is keeping many movie houses open, but
this is no reason to sit through a dull movie just to
enjoy America's favorite "munch." There now is
available in every market popcorn packaged in its
own aluminum foil skillet ready to put on a hot
burner, shake about a bit, and pop. An ingeniously
folded foil cover unfolds as the corn pops, and when

it has ballooned fully the corn is ready—even to the butter—and all you have to do is tear open the foil and eat. Try adding your own touch. For example, pour the hot popcorn into a bowl, sprinkle generously with grated Parmesan cheese, toss, and serve. Or melt 4 tablespoons of butter, add 1 teaspoon of curry powder, pour over the popcorn, toss, and serve with martinis-on-the-rocks.

If you do not like popcorn, but can't resist the urge to try your hand at popping it, then string it—using a darning needle and coarse thread—and hang it on your Christmas tree.

There is another type of corn which is served up once a year here in Bucks County. This is the revue presented each fall at the New Hope Annual Street Fair for the benefit of the Fire Department. The local hams write the script, compose the songs, make the lavish costumes, rehearse and rehearse. Result: corn of the highest caliber, to be enjoyed heartily for three nights only.

⤙ III ⤚

ODETTE AND
THE CASSOULET WAR

Odette Myrtil—the one and only Odette Myrtil, well remembered for her many Broadway roles, her forty-odd motion pictures, her supper-club and vaudeville appearances—I now like to refer to as "the successful actress who made good."

Starting her career in France as a violin prodigy, Odette played in many cities on the Continent. At seventeen she went to London, where it was discovered that she had not only a deft flair for comedy but a truly wonderful singing voice as well.

It was there that Charlot, the impresario who brought Beatrice Lillie and Gertrude Lawrence to our shores, engaged the young Odette for one of his revues. And it is not exaggerating to say that overnight she became the "toast of London."

She did not linger long in London, for an enterprising American impresario saw her there and brought Odette and her Stradivarius to New York, where her enviable career began in earnest.

Being French, Odette instinctively knows a great deal about food. When I asked her once where she actually learned to cook, her answer was typically amusing as she said, "On my bed at the Ritz in Boston." I hasten to explain.

When the *Red Mill* company was in Boston, where they played for several weeks, Odette was one of the few actresses permitted the privilege of staying at that very proper hostelry, the Boston Ritz.

Each night after the performance Odette invited eight or ten members of the cast to her room for a lobster-and-champagne supper. The lobsters were cooked each day at a fish market down on the wharf which Odette had discovered on one of her frequent walking tours. They were sent to the hotel, where the stage-struck young Room Service captain brought them to Odette's room after each performance . . . together with lettuce, hearts of celery, artichoke hearts, freshly made mayonnaise, French bread, etc.

The huge antique salad bowl which Odette had bought at a shop near the Common was placed on the bed, and the ceremony of preparing lobster salad became a nightly ritual.

Learning to cook by making lobster salad every night is rather like learning to play the piano by practicing "Chopsticks" for four hours each day, so I take this explanation with salt to taste. But, be that as it may, Odette does indeed know how to cook, and with that flair brought off only by the French.

Ten years ago Odette bought a charming old house here in Bucks County, and shortly afterwards she was approached by the owners of the Playhouse Inn in New Hope to act as manageress. The Inn was already set up with Polynesian cuisine, and Odette now laughs over the fact that not only did she not know anything about running a restaurant, but she hated Culinaire Chinois.

But she learned by trial and error, and soon the Playhouse Inn was *the* place. People came from New York, Trenton, Wilmington, Philadelphia; and in summer many tourists from all over flocked to the Inn. Odette stayed on for four years, and her experiences would make a fascinating book, including, as they did, everything from running out of beer at the brewers' convention to falling over her pet poodle and ending up in the hospital with a broken neck.

Then the theater beckoned once more, and Odette took a sabbatical and went into the lavishly produced musical *Saratoga,* which, unfortunately, was not a long-run hit. Odette's superb sense of timing stood her in good stead, however, and when she returned to the country the River House—an inn built in 1749—was available. Odette bought it, and now, some five years later, it is easily the most successful restaurant in the county. It is called Chez Odette, and many of the less sophisticated local people call Odette "Shay," which amuses her no end. Indeed, she sometimes refers to herself as "Shay."

The slogan of the restaurant is "Everything is 'Teddibly' French," and that it is. Well . . . for the most part. Odette has created a marvelous ambiance reminiscent of an inn you might come upon in the countryside of her native France. Most of the food is Odette's own creation, and it is all excellent. Consequently, the place is deservedly a *must* on everyone's list of places to go in Bucks County.

The menu at Chez Odette features unique appetizers such as Moules in Curried Mayonnaise, served ice-cold and superb. So easy to do, also, but it took Odette to think of it. And SHRIMP À L'OIGNON—the shrimp cooked in white wine with a bouquet garni, peeled, deveined and slit lengthwise, then rings of onions and homemade mayonnaise . . . all mixed together and chilled overnight. Incroyable! Les Escargots here have more flavor, more wine, and perhaps more garlic than anywhere else; and many of the regular guests now order them by the dozen, aswim in the hot butter. Odette's Onion Soup is perfection also, as is her Cream-of-Watercress Soup.

Odette has Langouste flown from France, and it is a featured item on the menu together with Imported Dover Sole. Each evening two or three Spécialités de la Maison are featured. For example: Monday—Cassoulet; Tuesday—Sirloin de Boeuf Chasseur; Wednesday—Mama's Chicken (roasted in so much butter the imagination staggers); Thursday—Gigot d'Agneau served with garlic-and-herb-flavored flageolets; Friday—Filet of Sole Bonne Femme; Saturday—Beef Bourguignon and Coq au Vin.

On Friday and Saturday, Roast Prime Ribs of Beef with Yorkshire Pudding is always on the menu, as a concession, Odette explains, to her great love for England, where her career was launched. Of

course the fact that it is a good "seller" is, I am
sure, incidental.

The day I enjoy most at Chez Odette is Sunday,
when the restaurant is closed and a few fortunate
friends are invited to Madame's charming house ad-
jacent to the restaurant, where she presides at her
own range. Every meal is a gastronomic delight, but
one thing I especially enjoy is PIGEONS ET CHOU-
CROUTE.

Odette sautées 6 squabs in butter with a small
amount of olive oil added, along with slivers of garlic and 3 or 4 chopped shallots. They are then placed
in a casserole, and 1 quart of drained sauerkraut is
heated in the pan and stirred to coat it with the
butter and seasoning. This is put atop the squabs,
and a pint of champagne poured over all. The casserole is covered and put into the oven for an hour
while the guests are served drinks.

The meal is completed with POMMES PARISIENNES
—small pre-cooked potatoes sautéed in butter until
well browned, then well sprinkled with chopped parsley.

Occasionally the Farberware Broiler is brought
into the dining end of the living room, and thick
steaks are broiled. No fuss, no bother, and—miracle
of miracles—no smoke. (I don't understand the
principle of this broiler, but then I don't understand
the telephone or electric lights.)

With the steaks Odette again serves Parisienne
Potatoes, this time embellished by adding at the last
moment canned (not frozen) artichoke hearts. Han-

dle with care, as these are fragile. The best ones are imported, and most good markets have them under various brand names.

It is a definite advantage when entertaining to own a fully stocked restaurant. When guests drop in, Odette has only to get the keys to the refrigerator and in nothing flat she can whip up cold lobster with homemade mayonnaise, or Caneton Bigarade avec Riz Sauvage, served with Endive Braisée, Asperges Vinaigrette, and Mousse au Chocolat.

Odette's Mousse au Chocolat is made daily with only imported Menier chocolate, the freshest eggs, and local whipping cream. The Babas au Rhum and the Profiteroles are made fresh each morning also, and Meringues Glacées are extremely popular, served with a choice of chocolate or Melba sauce.

The cave at Chez Odette is the most complete in the vicinity, and the wine sales are on a par with New York's best French restaurants, as Odette has educated her clientele in the joie de vivre et de vin.

Odette and I enjoy discussing food almost as much as we enjoy eating it. Occasionally the subject of cassoulet comes up, and then the battle is on, for she and I have definite, though contradictory, ideas about this peasant dish. She has her version; I have mine. And the twain almost meet.

Cassoulet is an ancient one-dish meal which originated in France. Languedoc, a province located in southern France starting with a wide sweep of the Mediterranean and extending back into the hills north and west, is famous for cassoulet—the one dish, incidentally, which my friends seem to associate most readily with my own kitchen. Other than Toulouse, the capital, the most famous city is the magnificently restored Carcassonne citadel, a mecca for tourists. One frequently hears the phrase ''See Carcassonne and die,'' but don't. Instead, relax in its ancient ambiance and be magically transported back seven hundred years into the thirteenth century. An overnight stop at the Hôtel de la Cité inside the fortress-like walls of the citadel is a unique experience that will forever remain a high point of anyone's first visit to France. And it is as good a place as any to begin a comparative tasting tour of the various versions of this famous one-dish meal.

Like many so-called gourmet dishes, cassoulet began life as a peasant concoction. Beans were not only inexpensive, but plentiful, and you could add almost anything that was around the kitchen. The thirteenth-century grandmères would surely never recognize their old mess of pottage if they saw the embellished and glorified results of today's added touches.

Cassoulet de Castelnaudary is the classic version and the one most appreciated by gourmets, but we will concede that other cassoulets have their merits.

The basic ingredient is dried white beans, but here it is only fair to tell you that American navy beans—while usable—do not produce the same effect. If you cannot find French dried beans, you should use white kidney beans, available at most importers of Italian foodstuffs. I use green flageolets because I find them easily obtainable from an Italian market on East 59th Street in New York, and the taste is ideal; but I will admit that one should use white beans to be truly authentic.

At the risk of sounding like a food-dropper, may I say that I have eaten cassoulet at the Grand Hôtel Fourcade in Castelnaudary, at the Hôtel de la Cité in Carcassonne, and at the Restaurant Richelieu in Toulouse. By far the best I have ever eaten, however, was at the Rôtisserie Périgourdine, situated at 2 Place St. Michel in Paris, just across the square from Notre Dame. The glass-enclosed rôtisserie is a work of art, and one can watch the chefs tending the meats on the spits while one relaxes in the charming dining area. The glass partition keeps the heat from coming into the cool salle à manger, while its highly polished brass frame reflects the immaculate fastidiousness of the patron.

A lavish portion was set before me—bubbling in its casserole—but so lavish indeed that I was certain the waiter thought I was expecting two or three guests to join me. I am delighted that this was not the case, and that the garçon was not in a hurry. He permitted me to savor and thoroughly enjoy all the nuances of this classic concoction.

It was cooked to perfection, and I have learned, regrettably, that this is not always the case in restaurants. I do not understand why restaurateurs allow their chefs to put cassoulet on the carte if the preparation must be rushed, or if it must be reheated too often. (I am in no way opposed to reheated cassoulet, provided care is taken to keep it moist and to heat it slowly. Let the guest wait. If he truly loves cassoulet, he will not object; and the extra time permits the taste buds to prepare themselves.)

Cassoulet de Castelnaudary

To make generous servings for 4 or 6 you will need:

> *2 pounds dry white beans*
> *6 quarts water*
> *1 pound salt pork*
> *¼ pound smoked bacon*
> *5 cloves garlic*
> *½ teaspoon thyme*
> *salt*
> *2 tablespoons mixed pickling spices*
> *1 pound fresh garlic sausage*
> *2 pounds lean pork*
> *2 legs and 2 thighs of confit d'oie*

Soak the white beans in water to cover overnight. In the morning drain and put them in a kettle with 6 quarts of water, the salt pork, the smoked bacon, garlic, and the thyme, and salt to taste. Put the mixed pickling spices in a piece of gauze, tie it up securely and add it to the pot. Boil slowly for approximately 1½ hours.

Meanwhile, grill the fresh garlic sausage, then remove from the pan and add the pork, cut in cubes. Sauté until lightly browned. Reserve the juices in

the pan. Into a casserole put a third of the beans, in
the center place 2 legs and 2 thighs of confit d'oie,
the cubes of pork, and the grilled sausages. Cover
with the rest of the beans and the juice. Bake in a
very slow oven at least 4 hours. Add a small quantity
of consommé occasionally to maintain the proper
amount of liquid.

From this has come a long line of variations, not
only in various parts of France, but also here in the
United States, where several of the excellent cooks I
know each has his or her own formula. Some of these
are superb, but others, I'm afraid, leave a great deal
to be desired. And this includes not only those of
cooks who are well-developed amateurs, but of some
professionals as well, up to and including chefs de
cuisine of major restaurants and hotels.

There are in New York at least three excellent
French restaurants where I always find superior
food—with the exception of their so-called cassoulet.
They really would do well to keep it off the menu.
Indeed, in some cases it turns out to be not even good
baked beans. And they have the effrontery to charge
as much as $5.95 for an à-la-carte order of what
turns out to be navy (U.S.) beans, salt pork, and
second-rate commercial sausage or—in one particularly shocking instance—even "hot dogs." Now,
really!

A friend of mine, Robert Gilfillen, makes an excellent cassoulet. He can't be persuaded to do it too
often, and I don't blame him, as it takes an enor-
mous amount of preparation, and "Gil" is a

perfectionist . . . even though he sparingly uses tomatoes in his version.

I have read dozens of recipes for cassoulet, and although I've never tried it, Craig Claiborne's sounds like one of the best. After all, his renown as the Food Editor of *The New York Times* as well as his personal reputation as a superb cook would certainly indicate that he knows what he is talking about when it comes to this painstaking dish.

Here in America our geese are not browbeaten and forced (literally) to eat, so it is difficult even to approximate the confit d'oie of Europe. Of course, you may buy confit d'oie here, but it is prohibitive in price. My friend Marc Ramniceanu, who is from Bayonne just outside Biarritz, gave me a marvelous tip on what is such a good substitute that it is almost better than the original. For DUCK RAMNICEANU, select 4 or 5 very plump Long Island ducklings (and if Long Island ducklings are not available in your town, use local ducklings. And someone please tell me why everyone calls ducks "ducklings").

Cut the ducks into quarters (this is easily done with a good pair of game shears). Sauté them, or even better, roast them very slowly with low heat for 3 hours, seasoned with salt, pepper, rosemary, and onions. Uh-uh, don't throw away the fat.

Place the cooked pieces of duck in a large stone crock of sufficient size. (I always remove the bones from the breast, but leave the leg and thigh bones.) Cover the ducks with the reserved fat which you have strained. There should be enough to cover the ducks completely, and if you are short you can add enough melted vegetable shortening to seal up the top. Permit this to stand in a cold place (or the refrigerator if you should have space) for at least 3 weeks—and longer if possible.

Then, when you make a cassoulet, remove the amount of duck you require, heat in the oven slowly to remove the clinging fat, and add the preserved duck to the cassoulet just before putting it in the oven. C'est bon! Later on we will talk about a dish in which you can use the duck giblets.

Since cassoulet requires a 2-day preparation period, I usually plan to serve it when I am inviting 15 guests, and that, I can assure you, is not too often. This is my method of preparation, and you will see that I have used what I think is the best of several versions I have enjoyed.

CASSOULET FOR FIFTEEN GUESTS

3 pounds green flageolets
3 plump ducks (or preserved ducks)
3 pounds boned shoulder of lamb
2 pork tenderloins
1 pound pepperoni
3 shallots, chopped
salt and coarse ground pepper
1 teaspoon dried basil
1 pound salt pork, sliced
2 onions, chopped
3 garlic cloves, chopped

87

> 1 level teaspoon of each:
>   white pepper
>   bay leaves, chopped
>   thyme
> ½ pound sweet butter
> 2½ pounds garlic sausage
> 2 cups white wine

The day before making the cassoulet, I roast the lamb and the pork tenderloins (or 3 pounds of pork-loin roast if the tenderloins are not readily available). I have also found that 1 pound of pepperoni adds an especially good flavor. I season the meats with the chopped shallots, garlic, salt, cracked black pepper, and the dried basil. Roast about 1½ hours at 400°F., remove from the oven, and cool overnight, covered. At the same time (the day before), I soak the green flageolets in cold water, and let stand overnight.

In the morning I drain them, and put them into a large kettle with the sliced salt pork (which I have scalded quickly to remove some of the salt), the onions, garlic cloves, white pepper, chopped bay leaves, and thyme. Cover with cold water and bring to a boil. Skim off the foam, and then add the sweet butter. Boil gently for 1 hour, and then add the pepperoni and simmer until the beans are tender.

When the beans are cooked, I put the pieces of preserved duck (one quarter for each guest) into the oven to heat. To serve 15 hungry guests you will need 2 casseroles (earthenware), of 6-quart capacity.

Fill the casseroles, starting with a layer of beans, then a layer of the garlic sausage (sliced ½-inch thick), a layer of pork tenderloin, sliced, and a layer of lamb, sliced, then the duck pieces, and, finally, another layer of beans. Pour a cup of white wine over the top. Place the casseroles in an oven set at 300°F., and bake for about 6 hours. After the first hour, a crust will have formed on top. Remove casseroles from oven, and gently stir this crust into the cassoulet. One ancient recipe written down for posterity by Anatole France suggests that this process be repeated 6 times, so there you are—the 6 hours of cooking time.

Do not permit the cassoulet to dry out. I save the juice from the beans, and mix it with the drippings from the roaster, to which I add another cup of white wine, and use this to add when more liquid is required during the baking period.

Odette prepares her cassoulet by the following recipe, which you can compare with mine. There is not too much difference, but each of us likes to feel that ours is the best. ODETTE'S CASSOULET serves 8 or 10 amply.

> *2 pounds dry white beans*
> *3 pounds lamb, cubed*
> *½ cup sweet butter*
> *½ cup olive oil*

6 cloves garlic
6 shallots
6 medium-size onions
1 tablespoon thyme
12 peeled fresh tomatoes or
2 cans Italian tomatoes
2 ducks
2 pounds French sausage (Toulouse saucisson)
several slices salt pork

Soak the beans overnight. In the morning boil them until the skins will peel off easily when you blow on them (about one hour of rapid boiling).

Meanwhile sauté the lamb cubes in butter and olive oil in a heavy skillet. When the lamb is well browned, remove it, and to the fat in the pan add the garlic, shallots, and onions, all chopped, and the thyme. Stir until lightly browned. Then add the peeled tomatoes, or 2 cans of tomatoes, drained.

Cut up the ducks and discard the backs and necks. Add the breasts and legs to the skillet, and sprinkle generously with pepper and salt. Cover and cook for 30 minutes over a low flame.

Now combine the beans with the lamb, duck, and sauce in layers in a large casserole, alternating the various ingredients and adding 2 layers of Toulouse saucisson (from Molinari's, a wonderful shop on Ninth Avenue in New York which features many imported foods).

Cut thin slices of uncooked salt pork and place on the top so that it is completely covered. Place the casserole in an oven set at 275°F. and bake for at least 4 hours—although 6 hours is much better.

Remove the casserole from the oven and sprinkle the top with a generous coating of seasoned bread crumbs. Place under the broiler for 5 minutes. Serve at once.

When serving cassoulet, bear in mind that this is a hearty dish. If you feel you must serve something first (I do not), make it a clear soup—preferably a mushroom bisque. A salad with a good cheese is perfect after the cassoulet. Or, if you are the dessert type, make it just a bowl of fresh fruit.

Personally I prefer a Pouilly Fumé with this meal, but a good Bordeaux is fine also. Many of my guests request beer, and that is not a bad idea.

Of course bread is a *must,* but it is also a *must* to serve small crusty rolls, or crisp French bread. None of this doughy commercial bread. And please: no butter. Instead, use the bread—as the French do—to sop up the juices.

And now, finally, I think I have heard (or read) everything, having just found a recipe for "French Cassoulet" which uses leftover lamb, salt pork, bouillon cubes, and *lentils.* This must surely be the Alsace-Lorraine version, via the home economist of a remote high-school cafeteria in Appalachia. But, wait a minute! Marian Tracy in her excellent book *Two Hundred Main Course Dishes* has topped it all with a recipe for cassoulet using *black-eyed peas.* Obviously Lady Bird's influence.

Finally, indeed. One last word: perfect your own

version of cassoulet—this most versatile, satisfying, tantalizing dish—and become known for your culinary prowess. Cassoulet takes time, effort, loving care, and some skill; but it is infinitely worth every single step necessary for its proper preparation.

~ IV ~

SOUP'S ON

Every European country has a notable soup for which it is famous:

> *Russia—Borscht*
> *Germany—Split Pea*
> *England—Mulligatawny*
> *Scotland—Scotch Broth*
> *Ireland—Barley Beef*
> *Spain—Gazpacho*
> *Greece—Lemon*
> *Italy—Minestrone*
> *Denmark—Fruit*

France is most famous for onion soup as served at Les Halles, but each province has its own soup of renown. Marseilles is known worldwide for bouillabaisse; Provence for garlic soup, which when properly concocted is like a yellow cloud and not at all the consistency we generally expect soup to be; Normandy for various potages; and Brittany for fish soups.

Vichyssoise is as French as soup can be, although

created in Manhattan by a Frenchman (Louis Diat at the old Ritz-Carlton) and first served to Charles Schwab, then later exported from America to France. That's a twist!

By the same token, chowders, for which New England is famous, originated in France. The fishermen of the French coastal towns hundreds of years ago added a portion of their catch to "la chaudière"—a large copper pot which was placed over an outdoor fire—and the townspeople shared the aromatic stew. Gradually the ingenious French cooks improved upon it by adding herbs and vegetables. In Normandy, where cream is used in practically everything, it was only natural to add it to the broth in la chaudière. Voilà! Fish Chowder.

We Americans are fortunate indeed to have inherited from all the world the best in culinary art, but somehow we manage to bastardize many of our legacies. For example, I once spent ten days on Cape Cod and each day I ordered New England Clam Chowder in a different restaurant. Result: ten different versions—some excellent, some fair, and two revolting.

New England Clam Chowder is one of my favorite soups, and so simple to prepare that I don't understand how it can go wrong so often. When I make it for a group of 8 or 10, I use 4 dozen clams, which I scrub under running water and put into a kettle with 2 cups of water (please, no salt). Cook, covered, over a brisk flame until the shells open. Remove from the stove, and set aside to cool in the broth.

I peel and chop 4 good-size onions. Dice ½ pound

of salt pork and sauté it in a heavy skillet until the cubes are dry and well browned. Drain on a paper towel and to the fat in skillet add the chopped onions and sauté over a low flame—don't let them burn.

Peel and dice 6 medium-size white potatoes, and boil them in enough water just to cover. Drain and reserve the water. Now remove the clams from their shells (discarding the shells), but save every drop of the broth. Strain it through a fine cloth. Cut up the clams with a knife. (Don't chop them fine, please.)

To the fat in the skillet add 2 heaping tablespoons of flour and 1 scant tablespoon of cornstarch (this keeps the finished chowder from curdling). Blend, and to this roux add the clam broth, plus the water in which the potatoes were cooked, and cook until it starts to thicken. Then place in a kettle, add the clams, 1 quart of milk and 1 pint of cream. Cook over a low flame, stirring constantly until thickened. Do not let it boil. Add the potatoes and cubes of cooked salt pork, plus a generous teaspoon of thyme. Keep hot—but do not boil—until ready to serve. Pass a basket of chowder crackers. Your 6 guests will hate you because you did not make more.

FISH CHOWDER is prepared much the same way, substituting cod, halibut, or mackerel for the clams. If you do not use salt pork in cooking, forget the clam chowder entirely, but you may substitute butter in the fish chowder.

MANHATTAN CLAM CHOWDER is not exactly my plate of soup, but there are those who like it in all its many versions. Some of them are merely vegetable soup with minced clams added. There is one true and original version, however, and it's not bad, I must admit.

Proceed with the clams in exactly the same manner and amount as described above. No salt pork in this, but the chopped onions are sautéed in butter and the flour is added when the onions are done to make the roux.

Meanwhile, chop 2 green peppers and 2 red peppers, and parboil them slightly. In summer, use 8 or 10 peeled fresh tomatoes, and in winter a large can of Italian peeled pomidori (tomatoes, prego). Add these to the peppers and bring to a boil. Pour the clam broth (if you do not have a quart, add enough water to make a quart) over the roux and allow to thicken slightly. Put the tomatoes, peppers, and clams into the soup kettle, add the thickened clam broth, and stir until it comes to a boil. Add a generous pinch of thyme. Now you *could* put in diced potatoes, carrots, and peas . . . but please don't.

Let's go back and start with our list now.

Russia—Borscht. Of course Poland, Romania, Yugoslavia, and Czechoslovakia all have Borscht, but to me it is Russian. Also, like all soups, it is peasant in origin, and I can just see the Russian peasants on the steppes with their beets and cabbages growing side by side awaiting harvest in the original Borscht Circuit. Borscht is not Borscht without cabbage. ("Borchok," which was served at the Russian Imperial Court, was made without cabbage, and was a strained beet soup to which the Czar and Czarina added Madeira wine. They sipped this with dainty slices of black bread, washed down with champagne. They had had their vodka earlier with half-sour dill pickles.)

To prepare sufficient Borscht for 8 you will require the following:

2 quarts beef stock (or 6 cans beef broth)
1 small head of cabbage, shredded
2 large onions, chopped
1 medium-size can peeled tomatoes
4 cloves garlic, minced
1 crumbled bay leaf
¼ cup sugar
1 generous teaspoon Hungarian paprika
juice of 3 lemons
grated rind of 1 lemon
12 medium-size fresh beets, cooked and chopped or
*   2 cans French-cut beets*
2 cups beet juice
1 cup chopped parsley

Combine all the ingredients except the beets and cook gently for 1 hour. Then add the beets and the beet juice. Cook 10 minutes, then add the cupful of chopped parsley. Serve in heated bowls. Pass sour cream and the pepper mill.

This soup is also delicious when served ice-cold on a simmering summer day.

PEA SOUP is as German as the Kaiser and Queen Victoria, but the French-Canadians in Quebec have their version also, made with yellow split peas, and mighty good too. This can be purchased in cans under the label "Habitant" if you care to save time.

To make your own, use

> *a ham bone with some meat remaining on it*
> *1½ pounds green or yellow split (dried) peas*
> *3 onions, cut up*
> *3 large carrots, scraped and cut up*
> *1 cup chopped celery*
> *½ teaspoon thyme (optional)*
> *salt and pepper to taste*

Place all the ingredients in a soup kettle, cover well with cold water, bring to a boil, and continue cooking slowly (adding water from time to time if needed) for about 2 hours. Remove the ham bone and set it aside to cool. Put the other ingredients through a food mill. Cut off the bits of ham and add them to the soup. If you wish, you may add 1 cup of evaporated milk or light cream, but if you do, be careful not to boil the soup when you reheat it. Freshly made croutons—cubes of dry bread fried in butter—are delicious atop each serving, and there will be plenty of soup for 8.

The English brought home many new recipes from India, surely a welcome relief from the roast beef and Yorkshire pudding, the boiled mutton with caper sauce, and the ubiquitous Brussels sprouts.

One notable British import was MULLIGATAWNY, an ideal soup for a cold winter night. It not only warms the cockles, but sets your mind to the glory that was England's in the days of Kipling.

a 4-to-5 pound stewing chicken
2 onions, chopped
1 cup celery tops, chopped
3 or 4 juniper berries (optional)
salt to taste
cracked black pepper
1 cup diced carrots
1 cup diced green pepper
½ cup chopped onions
½ cup chopped celery
2 peeled and chopped apples
1 tablespoon curry powder
3 tablespoons cornstarch
¾ cup water
½ teaspoon nutmeg
1 tablespoon sugar
2 cups parsley, chopped

Boil a cut-up 4-or-5-pound fowl covered with water to which you add the 2 chopped onions, the chopped celery tops, salt, and a generous amount of cracked pepper. 3 or 4 juniper berries are fine also. Cook until the meat is fork-tender, and remove the pieces to cool. Strain the stock and return it to the pot. You should have about 3 quarts. To this add the carrots, green pepper, another ½ cup of onions, and the chopped celery. Boil for 30 minutes, then add the apples. Cook 10 minutes and add a tablespoon of curry powder mixed with 3 tablespoons of cornstarch and ¾ cup of water. Stir until slightly thickened. Add ½ teaspoon of nutmeg and 1 tablespoon of the sugar. Keep hot but do not boil. Pick the meat from the cooked fowl, dice, and add to the soup. Sprinkle each of the 8 generous servings with the chopped parsley.

While we are in the British vein, let's not, please, overlook Scotch Mutton Broth. My Scottish friend Donald Roy MacLean, who was Resident Manager of the former Sheraton-East Hotel, tells me—and emphatically—that the only Scotch thing from Scotland is served from a bottle. He even looks down his nose at Butterscotch; and he's from Inverness, so he must know. Consequently, I shall refer to this delicious soup henceforth as MUTTON BROTH AS MADE IN SCOTLAND.

Since mutton for some strange reason is not easy to find in American meat markets, I use lamb. It is not as pungent as mutton, so I believe it better suits most American tastes. To prepare enough for 8, have the butcher save the bones from the leg of lamb he is boning and rolling for you.

You will also need:

> *2 pounds stewing lamb*
> *1 handful celery tops*
> *2 large onions, cut up*
> *1 crumbled bay leaf*
> *6 whole cloves*
> *12 whole peppercorns*
> *salt to taste*
> *2 cups carrots, diced*
> *1 cup chopped celery*

1 cup chopped scallions
¾ cup barley

Place the stewing lamb and the bones in a soup kettle. Cover with cold water, and add the celery tops, onions, bay leaf, whole cloves, peppercorns, and salt to taste. Bring to a boil, skim the top, and continue boiling gently about 2½ hours. Strain and reserve the meat, which you dice and add just before serving. Return the stock to the kettle (you should have 3 quarts), add the diced carrots, chopped celery, chopped scallions, and barley. Cook until the vegetables and barley are tender—about 40 minutes. The barley will thicken the soup to the correct consistency. Add the meat, and serve garnished with chopped parsley. It is much better to prepare the stock for this and every soup the day before so that the fat which rises to the top can be skimmed off.

This Mutton Broth is served daily in winter at the Soup Bar in Lord & Taylor on Fifth Avenue. If you do not want to make it, enjoy a healthy portion of it there. Top off your one-dish lunch with their deep-dish apple pie with hard sauce.

In Ireland they do a barley soup made with beef. It's hearty, me lads, but perfect if you are spending time in the peat bogs.

Once en route to Italy on the Italian Line's S.S. *Cesare Augustus* we docked at Barcelona at 8:00 p.m. and were in port for six hours. A group of us took a walking tour, and about 11:00 p.m. we were hungry, despite a superb dinner earlier on the ship, so we stopped at an attractive outdoor restaurant. It was a hot July evening, and we decided to try the Spanish chocolate ice cream which one of our group had heard was fabulous. Our waiter looked askance when we gave him our order, but dutifully brought four huge portions of Helado de Chocolate. No sooner had he put it before us than the waiter at the adjoining table wheeled up beside us a girandole bearing a large bowl of GAZPACHO surrounded by ice and smaller bowls of appropriate cut-up vegetables and garlic croutons. We pushed aside the ice cream, summoned our startled waiter, and asked that he serve us instead this Spanish soup. Perfecto! The Gazpacho was superb, and this is the way it was prepared. (Hide the Waring Blendor, José.)

For 8 servings you will require:

> *8 large ripe tomatoes*
> *2 sweet red onions*
> *2 cloves garlic*
> *2 cucumbers, peeled*
> *1 cup celery*
> *1 cup seasoned bread crumbs*
> *½ cup olive oil*
> *1 cup dry red wine*
> *Tabasco sauce*
> *1 can consommé*
> *1 medium-size can tomato juice*
> *1 small can tomato paste*
> *1 tablespoon sugar*

Chop or cut up in very small pieces the 8 tomatoes, which have been scalded first in hot water and peeled. Chop the sweet red onions, the garlic, the cucumbers, and the celery. Mix all the vegetables in a large bowl (not metal) and add salt and pepper to taste. Sprinkle seasoned bread crumbs over the top. Blend together the olive oil, dry red wine, and a few drops of Tabasco sauce. Stir into the soup together with one can of consommé (undiluted). Now add the medium-size can of tomato juice into which you have blended the small can of tomato paste and the tablespoon of sugar.

Refrigerate for at least 4 hours. Serve in small bowls with a cube of frozen tomato juice in each.

Pass an assortment of cut-up (diced) tomatoes from which most of the seeds have been removed, diced cucumber, diced red and green peppers, chopped scallions, and sprigs of parsley. Don't forget the pepper mill. Croutons fried in a mild garlic-butter are served warm as the final fillip to this "salad of soups."

The Greeks are extremely fond of lemon, and their soup called AVGOLÉMONO is standard fare in all Greek homes . . . from the lowly fisherman's shack to the palace of King Constantine and Queen Anne. There is an exceptionally interesting Greek restaurant on Eighth Avenue in New York called Pantheon, where the lemon soup is unusually good. When I was taken there by some Greek friends I thoroughly enjoyed the soup, the lamb, and the bacalava, but I am sure I shall never acquire a taste for the Retsini wine, which is flavored strongly with resin.

To make Avgolémono for 8, use 2 quarts of rich chicken stock to which you add ¾ cup of well-washed raw rice (not the pre-cooked variety). Boil for ½ hour and put through a food mill. Beat 5 egg yolks until creamy and add the juice of 2 lemons plus the grated rind of another. Stir 2 cups of the hot soup into the egg mixture, and then add this to the soup in the kettle. Place over a very low flame, and stir until slightly thickened.

If you wish to serve this soup cold, remove from fire and cool slightly, then add a cup of heavy cream. Chill thoroughly and serve in iced bowls, garnished with a spoonful of sour cream and a thin slice of lemon. Hot or cold, it is a deliciously refreshing and unusual soup.

This reminds me—because of the egg yolks, I guess—of a marvelous GARLIC SOUP I had for the first time in Provence while motoring through France. Don't be alarmed, but to 3 quarts of rich chicken stock add *24 whole cloves of peeled garlic*. That's quite a start, isn't it? Boil for 1 hour, adding water if needed to retain the original quantity of stock. Strain out, and discard the garlic. Better still, crush the cloves in a mortar, and add 1 pound of oleomargarine, then store tightly covered in the refrigerator for future use in making garlic bread.

To make sufficient soup for 8, replace this highly-seasoned stock into the kettle, bring to a boil after seasoning with salt and white pepper to taste, stir in ½ cup of arrowroot mixed with water, and cook until the soup coats a wooden spoon.

Beat 6 (8 *are* better if you can spare them) egg yolks until frothy—stir 2 cups of the hot stock into

them, and then add to the slowly boiling soup. Beat
constantly with a wire whisk until mixture is thickened. Serve at once in soup plates in which you have
first placed 2 1-inch thick slices of warmed French
bread. Don't plan to go dancing with your best beau
afterward, unless he has shared this heavenly brew
with you.

While we are in the South of France, let's toot
over to Marseilles and gorge ourselves on
BOUILLABAISSE. This is another soup which many restaurants in America try, but seldom really conquer.
It's not the fault of the chefs, but the fact is we just
do not have the varieties of sea food, nor does our
sea food have the same flavor as that in Europe.

L'Aiglon Restaurant on East 55th Street in New
York does serve an excellent Bouillabaisse every
Friday, and it is as close to the orginal as you are
likely to find on these shores.

Here is a version you can make at home with the
help of the best fish market on your list. It's hardly a
soup to prepare for just you and your spouse; wait
till some Saturday after the football game and ask
15 or 20 friends to join you in this one. Make it the
Friday before, as it is a production, but it lends
itself well to standing overnight, waiting to be ever
so carefully reheated.

You need a large soup kettle—in fact, the larger
the better. And if everyone you invite accepts, and if
some of your friends are prone to bring along an
extra guest or two, perhaps you should use 2 kettles.

You will also need the following ingredients:

6 *leeks*

8 *shallots*

7 *cloves garlic*

3 *large onions*

4 *carrots*

1 *large can Italian peeled tomatoes*

1 *demitasse spoonful of saffron*

1 *cup chopped parsley*

1 *teaspoon chopped bay leaf*

thyme

1 *cup olive oil*

1 *quart dry white wine*

6 *whole lobsters*

2 *pounds shelled and de-veined raw shrimp*

1 *pound red snapper*

1 *pound sea bass*

1 *eel*

2 *dozen mussels*

2 *dozen clams*

1 *pound codfish or mackerel*

Chop the leeks, after discarding most of the tough green part, the shallots, garlic, onions, and carrots. Place in the kettle and add the tomatoes, saffron, chopped parsley, chopped bay leaf, and a generous pinch of thyme. Salt and pepper to taste. Add the olive oil, and the quart of dry white wine.

Remove the claws of the lobsters, add them to the pot, then cut the lobsters crosswise into 4 or 5 pieces and add. Next place the raw shrimp in the pot. Then add the red snapper, sea bass, and eel, all cut into serving-size pieces. Now add the well-washed and scrubbed mussels in their shells, the clams in their shells, and boil for 15 minutes. You may now add pieces of codfish or mackerel, and cook 5 minutes with the lid on securely. If you reheat on Saturday, do not allow to boil.

I like to serve this in large flat soup plates with a freshly boiled potato, lots of crusty French bread, and plenty of Pouilly Fumé to wash it down.

In Italy they serve CIOPPINO, and there is a waterfront restaurant in most coastal towns where this Italian Bouillabaisse is readily available. Basically it is the same as the French except, as usual, the Italians use many tomatoes, red wine instead of white, and omit the saffron.

One of my favorite soups is BOULA BOULA; and no, it did not originate at Yale. I frequently do a fast version of it for 4, using canned green-pea soup diluted with light cream, canned green-turtle soup well laced with dry sherry, and blending the two together. Heat carefully just to the boiling point, place in individual ovenproof bowls, top with whipped cream, sprinkle lightly with Parmesan cheese, and place under the broiler until the tops are brown. Serve it immediately with freshly made Melba toast.

The best Boula Boula I ever ate was at El Morocco in New York, but that at the St. Regis Hotel is also superior. The next best was prepared by Henri Heller, formerly the Executive Chef at the Sheraton-East. Not only is Henri a chef par excellence, but he allowed me—as Banquet Manager—to get away with serving complicated dishes on the menus for parties of as many as four hundred. No other chef in New York would have tolerated serving Boula Boula to more than twenty persons.

Actually, Boula Boula should be made with purée of fresh green peas (frozen ones will do very well, however). Whether or not you make any other kind of soup, do try CREAM-OF-FRESH-GREEN-PEA SOUP. It is a delectable joy, and perfect to serve at dinner when the main course is to be roast lamb.

To make generous servings for 6, use 1 quart of freshly hulled peas, or 4 packages of frozen peas. Cook them for 10 minutes in 2 cups of lightly salted water. Put through a food mill or sieve. Then make a roux using ¼ pound of sweet butter and 2 tablespoons of flour. Blend well over the heat, and add 2 cups of light cream. Stir until thickened. Now add the purée of peas, plus the water in which the peas were boiled. Salt and pepper to taste. If you wish to serve cold, add more cream to ensure the proper consistency when chilled. Serve with a paper-thin slice of unpeeled cucumber afloat in each cup, and a sprinkle of chopped chives. The pepper mill is passed, of course.

This reminds me of a creation of mine about which guests are usually most enthusiastic—CUCUMBER SOUP. Now for this you do need a blender, and these ingredients:

> *3 or 4 cucumbers*
> *2 cloves garlic*
> *3 scallions*

½ cup cold water
1 can condensed green-pea soup
1 cup cream
sour cream
curry powder

Cut up the unpeeled cucumbers. Place in the blender bowl, add the garlic, scallions, and cold water. Blend for 2 minutes at high speed. Mix with the can of condensed green-pea soup diluted with the cup of cream. Chill in the coldest part of the refrigerator. Serve in 6 iced bowls with a dab of sour cream, sprinkled with curry powder, atop each portion. The Russians serve Cucumber Soup, but theirs is cooked and consequently loses a great deal of the cucumber flavor. Try this one for luncheon on the terrace when the temperature is well up in the nineties. Pass the pepper mill—and palm-leaf fans if there is no breeze.

MINESTRONE, like so many Italian foods, varies with each province. I think I prefer the Milanese, but that is because I am not at the moment in Italy. When I am there, I prefer whichever version I am eating, be it in Venice, Rome, or at the Marina Piccolo in Capri. In the northern part of Italy you are likely to find the soup made with pork, and rice used in it instead of pasta. Some cooks use cabbage, others spinach, and in Genoa eggplant is frequently added. In the South, olive oil is used, and much more tomato and garlic.

Let's take a middle-province version, and you add

or subtract to suit yourself, for I feel that minestrone is foolproof. You just can't go wrong.

1½ cups dry white beans
2 quarts water
3 cans condensed beef broth
3 or 4 tomatoes
1 cup chopped onion
4 cloves garlic
1 cup chopped celery
1 green pepper
basil leaves or 1 teaspoon dried basil
handful of thin spaghetti
1 quart fresh spinach leaves
1 small zucchini
¼ cup olive oil
garlic powder
oregano
Parmesan cheese

Soak the dry white beans overnight. Drain and
place in a kettle with the 2 quarts of water and 3
cans of condensed beef broth. Boil for 1 hour, then
add the peeled and cut-up tomatoes, chopped onion,
garlic, celery, and green pepper (cut in small
pieces), and the fresh (or dried) basil. Cover and
simmer for another hour. Then add a handful of thin
spaghetti broken in small pieces, and the fresh spinach leaves. Cook for another 15 minutes. Just before
serving, add 1 small zucchini which you have sliced
but not peeled, and sautéed in olive oil seasoned with
a dash of garlic powder and a sprinkle of oregano.

Serve in soup plates with freshly grated real Parmesan cheese, and hot, crusty Italian bread. A bottle of Chianti should be passed around the table. Tiny, highly seasoned meatballs are wonderful in minestrone, and they (or slices of Italian sausage) make it a perfect main course dish for 6 guests.

The last soup on our list of European specialties is Danish Fruit Soup. If you care to try this, may I suggest you call S.A.S. and when you land in Copenhagen, get a cab and go to one of the many restaurants in the Tivoli Gardens. There you are sure to find Fruit Soup, especially if you decide to make the trip in summer. Personally, I despise Fruit Soup.

When I started this chapter, I made a list of soups which I know how to prepare. When the count was 105, I decided no one should know how to prepare that many of *anything,* and I decided, further, not to bore you with a recitation of all the various kinds.

However, there are some tips about canned soups that I would like to share with you. Many of the canned soups available today are so good that if they are "doctored up" a bit, they can become your very own special gourmet creations.

For example, try mixing 1 can of cream-of-chicken and 1 can of turkey-noodle, 1 can of light cream, and a sprinkle of curry. Excellent, easy to do, and your 4 guests will be impressed.

I for one will never again make my own black-bean soup. I have on hand 3 pounds of imported black turtle beans which I store in an apothecary jar in a conspicuous spot in the kitchen as a woeful reminder

Soup's On

of the last time I ventured to make this soup. What a mess . . . so, never again.

Instead, to make BLACK-BEAN SOUP I use the condensed canned version diluted with consommé and generously laced with dry sherry. It is ready in 10 minutes; and served garnished with a paper-thin slice of lemon and grated hard-cooked egg yolk, it brings compliments until they are embarrassing.

Try adding a small can of cream-style corn to 2 cans of chicken-rice soup diluted with 1 can of water and 1 cup of cream. Sauté a chopped onion and a diced apple in butter until slightly cooked but not browned. Stir this into the heated soup, together with ½ teaspoon of curry powder. Add a can of stewed tomatoes. There you are—BRUNSWICK SOUP for 6, and your reputation as a cook enhanced once more.

Or mix a small can of cream-style corn, to which you have added a chopped onion sautéed in butter, with 2 cans of frozen oyster stew. ½ cup of heavy cream, heat slowly, and there you are again— OYSTER-CORN CHOWDER for 4.

There is an excellent canned lentil soup, to 2 cans of which I suggest adding a tablespoon of cider vinegar. Slice 3 or 4 skinless frankfurters, sauté them in butter, and add to this soup. Even starting from scratch, you could hardly hope to make better LENTIL SOUP.

For a CLAM-MUSHROOM SOUP, why don't you heat 2 cans of cream-of-mushroom soup to which you have added 1 can of light cream? Do not allow it to boil!

112

Drop in 24 cherrystone clams. The fishmonger will
open them and remove them from the shells. Cover
and place on a very low fire for 10 minutes (again,
do not allow it to boil). Place small squares of
freshly made toast, generously buttered, in individual serving dishes, then ladle in the soup. Pass the
pepper mill. Your 6 guests will be enchanted.

Try preparing about a dozen or more silver-
dollar-size crêpes. Open and heat 3 cans of beef consommé, diluted with 1½ cans of water and a 1-ounce
jigger of cognac. Cut the crêpes in quarters (there
are still 4 in each dollar) and place in 6 heated consommé cups. Pour the hot soup over them, and place *Consommé*
one full-size crêpe on top. In France this is known as *Celestine*
Consommé Célestine.

Of course you can be really devilishly clever by
sautéing rings of onion (use about 4 medium-size
onions) in butter—gently so they do not break up. In
a kettle, heat 3 cups of canned chicken broth with 1
can of strained cream-of-mushroom soup and 1 cup
of cream. Add the sautéed onions, ½ teaspoon of
thyme, ½ cup of chopped parsley, and 1 tablespoon
of tarragon vinegar. Now see what you have done?
You have just made Tourin au Soupe à l'Oignon as
it is served in Tours. I hope your 6 guests are impressed.

When you are at your favorite Italian food store,
buy a pound of dried mushrooms. Then, when you
finally get up enough strength to make cassoulet,
reserve a smidgin of energy and make Mushroom
Bisque. It's easy. To serve 6, just heat 3 cans of beef

113

consommé diluted with 2 cans of water, and add ¼
pound of the dried mushrooms. Steep over a simmer
flame, but do not allow to boil. Add more water if
any steams away. After 1 hour, strain. Reserve the
mushrooms in a covered container in the refrigerator until you next make spaghetti-sauce or any dish
requiring champignons. Serve the soup in 6 consommé cups, and pass cheese straws. You can also
put a dab of whipped cream atop each serving, and
dust with curry powder. (By now you must suspect
that my best friend is in the curry-import business.)

I find canned Vichyssoise dull, insipid, and certainly not worthy of its justly famed name. However, once, in desperation, I use some, doctored up in
a unique manner and so disguised that none of my
guests realized it was from a can. We were 8, so I
used 3 cans of soup to which I added 1 can of cream,
and blended well with a whisk. Are you ready? I
then added ½ cup of each of the following: seedless
white grapes, tiny canteloupe balls, diced cucumber,
diced fresh tomato, and watercress leaves.

This was thoroughly chilled in the freezing com-
partment (I was in a hurry—actually it is far better
if you leave it in the refrigerator overnight). It
should be served in chilled cups, and each serving
topped with toasted slivered almonds. Pass the pepper mill and hot cheese straws. This is a perfect
luncheon for a hot summer day, or an ideal first
course for dinner on the terrace. I call this ANDALU-
SIAN GAZPACHO.

One other time guests arrived on short notice, and
again I headed for the canned Vichyssoise in the

refrigerator. I also had some cans of jellied madri-
lène. This time I added cream to the Vichyssoise,
then diced the madrilene and mixed the two gently.
Voilà! MADRISSOISE. This was served topped with
chopped fresh dill, and the ubiquitous pepper mill
was passed to the 6 guests, together with fingers of
toast spread with Gentleman's Relish mixed with
sweet butter.

It's Sunday morning, and you've just remembered
that in a mood of perhaps-too-jovial hospitality the
night before you invited those 6 people for brunch at
one o'clock. They are the martinis-on-the-rocks set,
so Bloody Marys are out. O.K., but what about a
first course? Ah! Naturally, and what else? BLOODY
MARIE SOUP. Mix 2 cans of tomato soup, 1 can of
clam juice, a dash of Worcestershire, a splash of
Tabasco, and, oh yes, *a pint of vodka*. Stir well, or
better yet shake thoroughly. Chill until time to
serve. Into your best consommé cups, and put a few
pieces of Brandywine mushroom bits on top. "First
course now being served."

Are you still looking for Helen Nickel's recipe for
CREAM-OF-GREEN-TOMATO SOUP? Well, here it is in
proportion for 6 guests.

Cook 3 large green tomatoes chopped quite fine (I
run them through a food chopper) in 1 quart of
boiling water with a teaspoon of baking soda. Drain
through fine sieve or cloth after they have boiled 5
minutes. Then boil the tomato bits about 15 minutes
in fresh water. Blend 2 tablespoons of melted butter
with 2 level tablespoons of flour and gradually add 2

cups of milk, or more if the sauce is too thick. Cook over a slow fire, stirring continually until it comes to a boil, and combine with the tomatoes. This may sound like a lot of trouble, but it really isn't, and, regardless, it's well worth the effort.

Recently some friends from New York were just passing through Bucks County, and stopped to say "hello." I was up to my knees in tulip bulbs that were eager to be planted while it was still October. I have learned that there is no real privacy in the country, our urbane friends assuming that we just sit around in our ole rockin' chair like Mildred Bailey, waiting for the city folks to pop in. (Actually, I should feel flattered that they want to see me.)

After two hours of Bull Shots, I was ravenously hungry, so in self-defense I insisted that the "drop-ins" stay for lunch. The larder was rather bare of things that could be prepared quickly. There were 4 or 5 cold baked potatoes I had saved for potato salad. Oh yes, and a couple of tins of Dinty Moore's Corned Beef. Now, what's in this bowl? Some leftover Cream-of-Green-Tomato Soup.

I opened both cans of corned beef, cubed the chilled corned beef, and put it in a large skillet with ¼ pound of butter. Then I peeled and chopped the 5 baked potatoes, and put them in on top of the corned beef. Over both I poured the Cream-of-Green-Tomato Soup—on went the lid, and over a low flame.

I scrounged around in the freezer and came up with 3 packages of Sara Lee Croissants, which were placed in the oven. Then I opened 2 cans of

French-cut beets and drained them thoroughly. Next I shredded a head of lettuce, tossing the beets and lettuce together in the salad bowl with mayonnaise thinned with vinegar and a little sugar added.

I now carefully stirred the "hash"—poached 2 eggs for each one of the four guests, and placed the eggs around the mound of hash on my best platter. The croissants were hot, and I uncorked 2 bottles of Beaujolais. MacIntosh apples and Comice pears together with Port du Salut cheese was the dessert. And now you must know what you can do with a little leftover Cream-of-Green-Tomato Soup. I call it GREEN FLANNEL HASH.

Grandmother Carver, a grand old lady who had been born in Maine on October 13, 1828, came to Carversville after her marriage to the scion of the family which gave our town its name. This recipe for NAVY-BEAN SOUP—her husband's favorite—was always served with big slabs of Johnny Cake. (Did you know that this was originally known as "Journey Cake" when travelers, long before the Jet Set, carried large quantities in their portmanteaus?)

1 pound navy beans
1 cup ground salt pork (lightly pressed down)
1 large onion (cut fine or ground with pork)
1 large clove garlic (chopped very fine)
pinch of dry ground ginger
½ teaspoon rosemary
pinch of ground thyme
1 cup tomatoes
¼ cup hard cider or apple jack

Soak the beans in water overnight. Rinse well. Cover generously with tepid water. Bring to a boil in a covered pot, push to the back of the stove and simmer 1½ hours (approximately). Add the ground pork, onion, garlic, ginger, rosemary, and thyme; also the tomatoes. Bring back to a quick boil, and again push back to a reduced heat and simmer about another 2 hours, or until the beans are done. Then add the cider or apple jack, and salt and pepper to taste. Never salt beans while cooking, as it makes the skins come off and the beans become hard.

While this soup is cooking (never let it boil over) watch it and add a little water now and then. Keep covered. Serve it generously to 6 hungry guests.

For MUSHONION SOUP we are indebted to Donald Kooker, the gentleman who makes Bucks County Walking Sticks. Write to Donald at Point Pleasant, Pennsylvania, and he will send you a brochure showing these handsome sticks which are fun to own and ideal to send as gifts to those friends who seem to have everything.

Since preparing this soup requires 7 hours, it is a good one to plan to do on a stormy day when you can't go out anyway.

"We make Mushonion Soup in a 6-quart iron kettle over an open wood fire. Coat inside of kettle with Mazola oil. Fill ¼ with water. Chop 4 garlic cloves. Cut 12 onions into ½-inch cubes. Chop 1 pound mushrooms. Add 2 beef bouillon cubes.

"Fill the kettle with water, cover and bring to a slow boil for 4 hours.

"Then add ½ pound blue cheese, and salt and pepper to taste. Add water and slow boil for 3 more hours.

"Serve in 8 cups—with martinis—while the main course is readying on grill."

This is the perfect spot to discuss my favorite soup, which I call CHICKEN SOUP À LA SAUCISSON, and which I learned about from my friend Odette Myrtil. I understand it is a popular soup in Scotland. You will need an old hen or rooster, which you stuff with highly seasoned pork sausage mixed with an equal amount of dry bread cut into small cubes, 2 chopped onions, 2 cupfuls of chopped parsley, and 3 eggs, all mixed well and seasoned with salt and pepper. Pack this mixture loosely into the cavity of the old bird and in the neck cavity. Sew up and tie the legs and wings. Place in a large soup pot with a tight-fitting lid. Add 1 gallon of water, 3 leeks, 3 onions, 6 cloves of garlic, and black pepper. Cover and boil slowly for about 4 hours, or until the bird is fork-tender.

Remove from the stove and allow to cool overnight. Then skim the accumulated fat from the top and discard. Strain the stock, and reheat slowly without boiling. Cut up the chicken and serve in large soup plates together with some of the stuffing and plenty of the aromatic broth. Crisp French bread is a must, so that your 6 guests may "dunk," and dunk they will.

OFF THE TOP OF MY RANGE

Have you ever felt carried away at a cocktail party and impulsively invited ten or twelve guests for dinner on, say, the following Thursday night? "Come at seven." Well, now you are in this mess, so let's get you out by telling you a few quick tricks I have picked up here and there—altered a bit to meet the need of the moment, and served up in style in the garden, on the terrace, at a highly polished Queen Anne table, on card tables before the fire, or on a two-hundred-year-old harvest table at "Carver's Mill" in Bucks County.

Scene I

The rule at my house is that all guests are served a first drink from the bar set up on the terrace in summer, or in the living room beside the fire in winter. From then on they are on their own, and I hope they will feel free to refill at their pleasure. They usually do.

With the drinks I like to serve one or several of the following, quantity depending on the guests or

120

on the dinner and how long the preparation will require.

From Au Bon Goût in Palm Beach, thanks to Betty Lyons' introduction, I have sent to me via air mail their justly famous Flying Saucers—huge circles (about 15-inch diameter) of wafer-thin dough baked until crisp and reminiscent of Chapatti, the unleavened bread served in India. I "goose them up" with various things—e.g., garlic butter applied with a pastry brush, the saucers then spread with Parmesan cheese and baked for 5 minutes in a fairly hot oven; or a generous brushing of Bagna Cauda (watch for this later) and a quick bake. One time I mixed tomato paste, sugar, brandy and fresh basil. This I spread lavishly on the saucers before popping into the oven. Or try them with a mixture of tunafish, anchovies, garlic powder, lemon juice, and olive oil whipped in the blender, then spread over the top before 5 minutes in a hot oven.

Of course you can mix Gentleman's Relish from Fortnum and Mason's with butter, and paint the saucers. Whatever you do, keep them frozen until you do it, and then when you have done it, bake them 5 minutes. They are of generous circumference, so use your chop plates to serve them, and suggest that the guests just break off a piece. This is easily done as they are très croustillant.

When time permits, I make what I call HOLIDAY MEATBALLS, and serve them in a chafing dish. Have the butcher grind the tips of a tenderloin (travel in a Brink's truck, for I assume you will really indulge and buy the entire filet de boeuf). You will also need:

> *Napoleon brandy (your best)*
> *salt and pepper to taste*
> *cooked wild rice*
> *2 eggs*
> *ground walnuts*
> *sweet butter*
> *3 or 4 juniper berries*

Mix the ground tenderloin tips with 2 tablespoons of brandy for each ½ pound of meat, salt to taste, a few grinds of the pepper mill, and a handful of cooked wild rice together with 2 egg yolks. Mix with your fingers, and shape into very small balls (about 36). Roll them in the ground walnuts, and sauté them in sweet butter to which you have added the juniper berries. Place the meatballs in a chafing dish which has already been well heated, add more brandy, and just before your entrance, light it—then whistle "The Song of the Flame" and in you go.

Does that really sound complicated? It isn't, but if you think so, why don't you plan instead to order from your favorite greengrocer several bunches of white icicle radishes. Just wash them well, cut off the root tips, and plunge them into icy water. Serve them in a bowl of shaved ice together with lightly salted butter which the guests spread on the radishes. It's a neat trick, and fun to watch.

Or for DATE-BACON APPETIZERS, soak pitted dates

for several days in Wild Turkey Bourbon. Then wrap them in bacon and broil until the bacon is crisp. Don't serve this if you have invited any members of the Temperance Union. In that case, stuff pitted prunes with homemade peanut butter and proceed as above. I am not kidding about the HOMEMADE PEANUT BUTTER. Buy 3 pounds of peanuts in the shell, roast them until they are well browned, shell, and remove the skins. Place in a Waring Blendor together with ¼ pound of melted butter and 1 level teaspoon of salt. 3 minutes at high speed and you will have a pint of delicious peanut butter. "Skippy," go home.

Del Monte will be eternally grateful if you will buy their pineapple chunks, open the can, drain, and soak them in Kikkoman Soy Sauce for 3 or 4 days. Then broil them, and our fiftieth state will be delighted it joined the Union.

Why don't you have your favorite delicatessen very thinly slice Scottish smoked salmon (or lox if you are feeling penurious), take it home and carefully spread each thin slice with Philadelphia Cream Cheese, which you have blended with sour cream and chopped watercress. Then roll into jelly-roll shapes, cut into 1-inch slices, and serve these SALMON-CHEESE ROLLS on a chilled silver tray with watercress garni.

Prosciutto can be done the same way, except use horseradish in the cream cheese. These are my favorite appetizers.

Then you have the more subtle type, such as tiny wedges of melon wrapped in razor-thin slices of prosciutto. This is especially good on a hot summer night.

Winter and the snows of yesteryear call for Caroline Davis' SAUSAGE ROLLS. Use your very best country sausage—which you were saving until the boss and his wife came for breakfast—sauté it, and drain on paper towels. Then prepare a very rich dough of Bisquick which you roll out into ½-inch-thick strips. To make the dough rich, use cream instead of the usual milk. Wrap the pre-sautéed sausage in the dough, jelly-roll style. Cut into 1-inch slices, then bake 15 minutes in a hot oven. Of course you arrange each slice on a well-greased cookie sheet before placing in the oven.

The BAGNA CAUDA mentioned earlier is the Italian answer to Switzerland and its ubiquitous fondue. In a heavy saucepan place 1 pint of olive oil to which you add 6 cloves of garlic, slivered, and cook slowly over a low flame until the garlic is brown but not dark. Then add 6 or 8 filets of anchovy, and wait until they more or less disintegrate. Transfer this smelly concoction to your best chafing dish, and have ready all sorts of cut-up vegetables such as: cauliflower florets, celery hearts, celeriac roots (anise root), endive, green pepper, cucumber, artichokes; or be ingenious and add your very own selection. These are dipped into the bubbling Bagna and popped into the mouth as extra thrills for the taste buds preparatory to dinner. Chinese pea pods which have been packed in ice are inordinately good with this.

Try putting in the freezer a large bunch of seedless white grapes wrapped in foil. Leave them at least a day (longer if you are foresighted), then serve them still frozen with cocktails. Far less calories than most tidbits, and especially refreshing when it is ninety degrees by the pool and everyone is panting from the heat.

Once in a while surprise your guests and don't offer the entire bar. After all, they are not at the Oak Room of the Plaza. But make your one drink interesting by serving, for example, only SAZERACS, the cocktail which made New Orleans—and especially Seymour Weiss's Roosevelt Hotel—famous. Ted Saucier has the original recipe in his wonderful book *Bottoms Up,* and if you follow his directions, Jean Lafitte couldn't do it better. Herbsaint (actually absinthe minus the wormwood which caused it to be banned not only in Boston but everywhere except perhaps Algiers) is not readily available at State stores, so use Pernod, which, I assure you, tastes almost the same.

Proceed in this manner. Into an old-fashioned glass pour 1 tablespoon of Pernod, swirl the glass to coat the sides, pour the excess liqueur into another glass, then place a cube of sugar in the bottom of the old-fashioned glass and splash it with Angostura bitters, muddle a bit, fill the glass with small ice cubes and pour in your best bourbon or rye up to the top. Run a lemon peel around the rim of the glass and serve. Limit: 2—maybe 3 for the really experienced drinkers.

Princess Kropotkin turned over to me her recipe for HAWAIIAN JACK, and it is good to drink . . . or to blow up the bridge over the River Kwai. Two parts 100-proof apple jack, one part unsweetened pineapple juice, the juice of ½ lemon, and 1 tablespoon of Rose's Lime Juice. Shake with lots of very cold ice—serve in a martini glass.

Bloody Marys and Bull Shots are fine before brunch, but somehow they seem too hearty as a drink before dinner. Why not make BLOODY MEDICIS, using 2 parts V-8 Juice, 1 part clam juice, 2 parts vodka, 1 part lemon juice, 1 part consommé, and a generous dash of Worcestershire sauce. I leave the amount of Tabasco entirely up to you. I usually add fresh basil leaves to each glass—it looks good and the bouquet is wonderful as you sip the drink.

What's wrong with MINT JULEPS? Nothing, I say, except they are a powerful lot of work if you prepare them properly, "suh." Sterling-silver mugs are, of course, best, because they frost quickly, but there was a bartender named Artie at the Sheraton-East who made excellent ones in a glass which frosted before your eyes as he stirred the drink slowly with a long bar-spoon. His secret was simple syrup—instead of sugar—plenty of fresh mint leaves (no stems) and very finely crushed ice. The Wild Turkey Bourbon helps, too. Picture yourself and your guests on the terrace or poolside, the day a sweltering one in August, and lunch an hour away. Bring on the Juleps, and serve some hot cheese straws coated with sesame seeds; or little beaten biscuits split and generously filled with thinly sliced "old ham"—the Kentucky kind, which is a fetish with Louisvillians. They just let it get old. *Moldy old.*

Scene II

Dinner? Oh yes, the guests were asked for dinner. Now let's take a tour of what I consider to be fabulous kitchens, and expose their secrets.

L'Aiglon—on East 55th Street in New York, diagonally across from the St. Regis—serves a classic Continental cuisine with an unusual flair, including BLANQUETTE DE VEAU, and this you must try when you are entertaining 8 special friends.

> *2 pounds breast of veal, cut in 2-inch cubes*
> *¼ pound salt pork, cut in ½-inch cubes*
> *1 cup dry white wine*
> *12 small white onions*
> *12 small mushrooms*
> *6 small carrots, cut in ¼-inch slices*
> *3 tablespoons butter*
> *¼ cup flour*
> *2 cups veal stock*
> *2 egg yolks, slightly beaten*
> *¼ cup cream*
> *1 tablespoon minced parsley*
> *1 tablespoon lemon juice*
> *grating of lemon peel*

Cook the veal and the salt pork, just covered with water and 1 cup of dry white wine, for 45 minutes, skimming as required. Add the onions, mushrooms, and carrots, and simmer until the vegetables are done, and the meat is tender but still firm. Put the butter in a saucepan with the flour. Cook gently until it bubbles. Add the veal stock, the cream, the lemon juice, and a grating of lemon peel, plus the parsley, and the egg yolks, slightly beaten. Cook till thick, but do not let it boil. Drain the meat, pour the sauce over it, and serve hot.

L'Aiglon's hospitable owners, Guido and Joseph, will not be happy, come July and August, should you pass up their truly marvelous VITELLO TONNATO.

I first had this Italian dish at a small trattoria in a mill town in Italy one hot August noon. I was served in the garden, and after the melone e prosciutto the waiter brought a platter of veal (icy cold) with tuna-fish sauce. Mama mia!

My method of preparation is not difficult, and yet, as you know, veal can be a problem when it is roasted, as it tends to become dry. Let's face it: in America we do not have the quality of veal that you find in Europe. However, be not deterred. Just call your butcher and order a 5-to-6-pound roast of veal, to be boned and tied. Place the veal in a heavy pot and sear over a hot flame. Now add 4 cups of chicken broth, 2 cups of dry white wine, a bay leaf, 4 chopped garlic buds, a handful of celery tops, 2 large carrots—cut up—and a bag of French's Crab Boil (a wonderful bouquet garni all ready to use—no hunting for gauze, etc.). Cover the pot and cook slowly on top of the stove for about 2½ hours. Remove from the fire and allow the meat to cool in the pot.

Now the sauce: Most recipes tell you to use a mortar and pestle, but the blender is much easier and does a superb job. Two cans of white-meat tuna-fish, 4 anchovies, 2 teaspoons of Dijon mustard, 1 teaspoon of garlic powder, 1 teaspoon each of powdered thyme, savory, salt, and freshly ground white pepper. Place all the above in the blender, add ½ cup of fresh lemon juice, turn on low speed and gradually add 1 cup of olive oil. Turn blender to high speed for 1 minute. Remove the sauce to a bowl and stir in ½ cup each of capers and chopped Italian parsley. Slice the cold veal and place it in a shallow dish which has a cover. Pour the sauce over the meat, cover, and put in the refrigerator for 2 days. Serve it as a first course at a dinner for 8, or as a main course at a luncheon for 4. A Soave white wine should be served with it. Pouilly Fumé is not bad either.

Why not CHICKEN TETRAZZINI? Madame Luisa Tetrazzini, the famous diva, adored spaghetti more than anything in the world, unless it was creamed chicken. An ingenious chef at the famous Delmonico's at the turn of the century enchanted her by serving Crème de Volaille atop spaghettini, sprinkled with freshly grated Parmesan and placed under the salamander until the cheese was browned and the sauce bubbling.

I have my own version in which I use green spinach noodles, well buttered and placed in the bottom of a casserole, topped with lots of cooked chicken in a rich cream sauce to which I add sherry. Then the Parmesan in generous quantity, and into the oven set at 400°F. for 30 minutes. When I feel particularly festive, I add thin slices of ripe avocado, which I have first marinated in French dressing, to the top of the noodles before the creamed chicken. Top that, Luisa!

Why don't you keep a constant supply of frozen patty shells in your freezer and always Be Prepared? After baking the patty shells according to the directions on the carton, remove the tops from each, and with a 3-tined fork remove and discard all the spongy dough. Return the shells to the oven for 5 minutes to dry and crisp.

For Eggs Vol au Vent, fill 6 of the shells with scrambled eggs and top with creamed bacon. Having cut the bacon into small pieces, fry until crisp, then drain on paper towels or dry bread. Add 1 cup of bacon to 2 cups of rich cream sauce, and sprinkle with chopped parsley. Hashed-brown potatoes and broiled tomato slices make an ideal accompaniment. (By the way, whatever happened to Alice Foote MacDougall?)

Ratatouille is known as a French dish, but I think it sneaked into their cuisine by way of Algiers or Morocco. Whatever its origin, it is an extremely pleasant concoction.

To prepare a sufficient amount for 8 or 10 guests you will require:

>   *4 large eggplants*
>   *6 medium-size zucchini*

2 tablespoons salt
4 large Bermuda onions
3 green peppers
4 or 5 garlic cloves
1 cup olive oil
2 large cans Italian peeled tomatoes
1 tablespoon thyme
3 crumbled bay leaves
1 tablespoon cracked black pepper

Peel the eggplants and dice them into 1-inch cubes. Slice the zucchini. Place both in a large bowl, add the salt, and mix well. Cover with a weighted plate for 1 hour.

Peel and slice the onions, seed and slice the green peppers very thinly, and chop the cloves of garlic.

Heat the olive oil in a heavy skillet, fry the onions until slightly browned, and add the garlic. Cook for 5 minutes, then add the 2 cans of tomatoes, from which you have drained most of the juice, and the thyme and bay leaves.

Meanwhile, drain the eggplant and zucchini in a colander, then place with the green peppers in a roasting pan with high sides. Stir in the hot mixture, adding a generous sprinkling of black pepper. Place in a 350°F. oven and stir occasionally, being careful not to break up the vegetables too much. Bake uncovered for 1½ hours.

This dish may be served hot or cold. I prefer it cold in lieu of the usual mixed salad on a summer buffet.

Sometime when you have leftover roast lamb, cut

it from the bone and mince it with a knife. For each cup of meat add 1 cup of Ratatouille. Place in a casserole, sprinkling seasoned bread crumbs generously over the top. Bake in the oven (350°F.) for about 30 minutes. Behold a MOUSSAKA as Romanian as Queen Marie.

RICE PANCAKES are a specialty of my friend Charles Darnell. He makes them frequently for Sunday breakfast at his Manhattan apartment, and when served up hot off the griddle with sausage patties, warm maple syrup and plenty of soft butter, they always make a hit, even with the most diet-conscious crowd.

To make enough pancakes for 6, boil 1 cup of washed long-grain rice in 2½ cups of salted water until the rice is tender. Do not drain, but stir in at once ⅛ pound of butter. Cool slightly, then add 4 eggs, a heaping tablespoon of sugar, 2 level teaspoons of baking powder, 1 cup of light cream, and enough flour to make a thin batter (about 1½ cups).

Bake them on a hot griddle and serve at once. Do not stack them. They are also excellent for lunch, with creamed chicken.

RISOTTO MILANESE is another easy thing to prepare. Try to find real Italian rice—most good Italian markets carry it. It is a more bulbous grain than the American kind, and cooks easily with no excess starch. Wash it and shake out all the moisture you possibly can. Sauté 2 cups of the washed rice in a heavy skillet with a tight-fitting lid. Use ¼ pound of butter plus ½ cup of olive oil to which you have added 2 cloves of thinly sliced garlic. Toss the rice with a spoon so that it is well coated with the oil and butter. Pour in 5 cups of strong chicken broth. Cover and cook 20 minutes over a medium flame. Check once in a while (but try not to stir) to be sure there is plenty of liquid—it cooks away too quickly on a damp or humid day. If you *must* stir, please do it only with a fork. When the rice is tender, salt to taste and grind in some black pepper. Serve with almost anything, to 8 people.

There are so many interesting additions you can use to make this into a main-course dish. Sautéed mushroom caps and chicken livers are excellent. Or sauté fresh-peeled and de-veined shrimp in butter for 5 minutes and add to the rice. Lobster meat sautéed in butter and flambéed with brandy, then added to risotto, is almost too good to be believed, and the guests weep for more. And, finally, prosciutto ham diced and sautéed quickly in butter, then added to the rice with an equal amount of diced Gruyère cheese. Toss slightly and serve before the cheese melts.

Here in Pennsylvania we are fortunate to find excellent DRIED BEEF. Some of the markets slice it razor-thin before your eyes, but the packaged type is usually very good also. This makes a wonderful brunch. (Joe Tankoos of the Delmonico Hotel in New York has announced the addition of "Bruncheons" to their overwhelming list of events.)

To prepare 6 generous servings, tear the dried beef into small pieces and sauté them in butter. I use

½ pound of beef to ¼ pound of sweet butter. Stir in 2 heaping tablespoons of flour, and add 3 cups of milk and 1 cup of cream. Continue stirring until the sauce thickens. Serve over scrambled eggs.

Or, better still, have ready CORNMEAL MUSH which you have prepared well in advance by cooking 1 cup of yellow cornmeal in 4 cups of salted water until thick. Remove from the stove, stir in 3 tablespoons of butter, and pour into a greased bread pan. Cool and refrigerate at least overnight. Cut into 1-inch-thick slices and sauté in butter. The creamed dried beef over this is a perfect marriage.

When you awaken one morning overwhelmed with ambition, just hope that this feeling will continue throughout the following day as well. Then, you are ready to make PETITE MARMITE. Call your butcher and order about 5 or 6 pounds of beef to boil (I use bottom-round) and a leg bone cut into 3-inch pieces. Ask him to send along 2 chickens as well. Call the greengrocer and order 3 pounds of small white turnips, 2 pounds of white onions, 1 dozen carrots, 2 small very firm heads of cabbage, 1 bunch of leeks, and another of celery.

As soon as the ingredients have been delivered, call 3 or 4 of your favorite couples and invite them to dinner the following evening, as there will be plenty for about 8 or 10 people.

Put away the meats and vegetables, and while you are about it check to be sure you have coarse salt (the kosher type is fine), some small gherkins, horseradish, and Dijon mustard.

If you hurry you will just make it to the club in time for nine holes. Whatever you do, be sure you arrange a simple dinner for this evening, and plan to retire early with a good cookbook.

The following day please get up early, as there is much to do. First, put the beef and the pieces of marrow bone (wrapped in muslin and tied securely), into a pot of sufficient size, adding 2½ quarts of cold consommé. Doesn't everyone have 2½ quarts of cold consommé around the kitchen? If you are one of the less fortunate and do not, use Campbell's. Bring to a boil and skim.

After 2 hours of slow boiling, add the turnips, carrots, leeks, and celery, all cut into small pieces. Blanch the 2 cabbages in salted water, and add them *whole*. Simmer very gently for 3 hours.

Meanwhile, roast the chickens in a slow oven together with their giblets—all seasoned well with salt, pepper, and 2 cloves of garlic.

Remove the pot from the stove and when the fat rises, skim off and discard. Return the pot to the stove and now add the chickens and giblets. Bring to a boil. Voilà! Petite Marmite.

To serve, place the meat (beef and chickens) on a large platter and surround it with the vegetables. The broth is placed in a tureen and can be served as soup first, together with French bread which you have dried out in the oven. Then the meat and vegetables are the main course, and here you serve the coarse salt, the gherkins, horseradish, and moutarde.

I like to serve the whole thing at once in large soup plates, giving each guest slices of beef, chicken, the vegetables, etc.

Remember, the salt is served—not cooked in the pot. I'm not sure it toughens the meat, but someone suggested a long time ago that it does, so we'll go along with that theory.

A vin ordinaire is very much in order with this. And if you must serve dessert, make it a simple one. Cheese—maybe a few pears—certainly bread, and more wine, followed by Café Filtre, and you are as French as de Gaulle or Toulouse-Lautrec.

Do you have a wood-burning fireplace? Wonderful. Why not make a JAMBON DE BAYONNE?

About September 15 order a 12-to-15-pound fresh ham. Blend together 1 pound of salt, ¼ pound of black pepper, and 1 quart of sifted wood ashes. Rub this mixture generously over the entire surface of the ham, then place it in a basket and hang in a cool place. Make a note on your kitchen bulletin board to remind yourself to bring the ham out of its hiding place every 3 days, wipe away the salt and ashes, then re-coat with the same blend. After 2 weeks you will note that the preserving mixture no longer becomes moist as most of the moisture from the meat has by now been absorbed.

Now you will need a burlap bag. Cut it in half, retaining the lower portion. Wash it thoroughly, rinsing it well. In a large kettle, place 3 gallons of water and 1 pound of salt, bring to a boil, and toss in the burlap bag. Boil for 10 minutes, remove the kettle from the fire; allow the bag to cool in this saline solution, then squeeze it dry and hang it in the sun. When thoroughly dry, place the ham inside, tie up securely, and hang in a cool place for 2 weeks.

Now call the hardware store and order a 12-foot length of heavy-duty link chain and two "S" hooks, one for either end.

Take your ham in its burlap cocoon, the chain with the hooks, a large cement nail, and a heavy hammer. You may need a helper to assist you up the ladder to the roof where you will drive the cement nail into the top of your chimney. Attach the chain, then lower the ham down the chimney on its chain until it is 3 feet above the fire level.

Follow your usual routine all winter, having fires whenever desired (please don't use cannel coal). Forget about the ham. You do not have to have daily fires; in fact, the ham does very well with occasional cooling-off periods.

About March 15 go up the ladder and retrieve the ham. Don't be unhappy when you see how black the burlap has become. Just remove it, then wash the ham with a mild solution of warm water and baking soda. It is now ready to eat, uncooked if you like. It is excellent when sliced wafer-thin and wrapped around wedges of Spanish melon. It would be a shame to use it for sandwiches, unless you make open-face ones on well-buttered black pumpernickel.

You can go very Basque if you care to, by serving thin slices of the ham, sautéed gently in butter, with PIPÉRADE. This is prepared by sautéing the following in sweet butter: 2 thinly sliced green (or red) peppers, 1 medium-size onion, also thinly sliced, and 4 peeled, sliced tomatoes. (Use a heavy skillet.) When this mixture is bubbling, add 6 whole eggs, 1 at a time, stirring with a fork. Season with black pepper and salt, and serve immediately to 4 lucky guests.

We still have those duck giblets in the refrigerator, so let us do an ABATIS DE CANARD EN FRICASSÉE AU BLANC. We can use abatis de dinde et de poulet also, together or separately.

Just be sure you have:

> *2 pounds giblets*
> *a few wing tips*
> *3 or 4 necks cut into pieces*
> *2 leeks*
> *½ cup chopped parsley*
> *3 cloves garlic (chopped)*
> *1 bay leaf*
> *4 whole cloves*
> *½ teaspoon thyme*
> *½ teaspoon basil*
> *1 heaping tablespoon flour*
> *1 quart chicken stock*
> *12 small whole mushrooms*
> *3 egg yolks (beaten)*
> *½ cup heavy cream*
> *vinegar*

Clean and wash the giblets, reserving the livers, and place in a saucepan together with the wing tips and the neck cut into pieces, add a generous amount of butter, the leeks, cut up, and the parsley, garlic, bay leaf, cloves, thyme, and basil. Salt and pepper, of course. Add a heaping tablespoon of flour, stir to coat the pieces, and moisten with the quart of rich chicken stock. Cook slowly until the gizzard is tender, then add the livers and mushrooms. Cook another 10 minutes, remove from the fire and strain. Return the sauce to the pan, reheat, and add the beaten egg yolks mixed with the cup of heavy cream. Stir constantly until thickened. Remove from the fire and stir in a dash of vinegar. Add the cut-up giblets and reheat but do not boil. Serve with plenty of bread to sop up the sauce. 6 hungry people will relish this and it is very easy to prepare.

My first experience with this was in Paris at the Restaurant Lyonnais, where I was the guest of M. and Mme. André Malvy. Had I not been, I doubt that I would have found the restaurant, for it is situated in what is more an alley than a street, near the Opéra, and the sign outside is surely one of the first electric signs ever made and has become rather faded, to say the least. However, the patron caters to a strictly French clientele, and the diners are a most impressive group made up mainly of men and women of the French literati. Here one is sure to find authors and playwrights together with their publishers and producers. A new sign would probably attract tourists, such as me, and thus drive away the "regulars" who consider the Lyonnais their special retreat.

Menus are available, I am sure, but no one ever orders dinner. The patron knows each guest, and serves him according to his particular taste or whim.

The Fricassée was a little extra tidbit served at our table since it is a special favorite of my host, M. Malvy. I respect his good taste. Try it and see if you do not agree.

My favorite restaurants are in Italy, one being the Antico Martini in Venice. Here, as an amusement for the American tourists, they do a DRUNK STEAK. A generous-size chafing dish with a hot flame is wheeled to the table, where the captain proceeds to melt a liberal amount of sweet butter in the pan. Then for each guest he quickly sautées 3 thin slices of beef tenderloin on either side, pours a whopping good splash of Scotch Whisky over the meat, and sets it aflame. The meat is then removed to a heated platter, and to the butter and pan-juices he adds a goodly quantity of Worcestershire, a few dashes of hot pepper sauce (Tabasco), and 2 or 3 large spoonfuls of Extrait de Viande (I use Bovril). Stir well to blend, and when it is bubbling hot add ½ cup of chopped parsley, and stir in 1 cup of heavy cream. Return the meat to the pan and heat it in the sauce.

I serve it with green noodles tossed in butter, cream, egg yolks, and Parmesan. An endive salad with garlic dressing is a perfect accompaniment.

Try doing chopped sirloin in this manner. It elevates it from the lowly hamburger classification to a rare gastronomic experience.

Ristorante Tre Scalini in the Piazza Navona is, I think, my favorite of all my favorite ristorantes in Roma. The food is all excellent, and the Gelato Tartufo, their special chocolate dessert, an event in itself. Probably the location appeals to me as much as the food as it is opposite the fabulous Bernini fountain, which to me is "high camp" at its best. The fact that the celebrated feud between the sculptor Bernini and the architect of the church opposite the fountain in the square took place several hundred years ago pleases my sense of the ridiculous.

Signor Bernini, the leading sculptor of his day, had been commissioned to create a fountain for the center of the piazza. At the same time a young architect had designed a church which was being erected across from the fountain. Bernini presumed to criticize the architect's innovation of a suspended dome, telling him that it would collapse if he did not add supporting columns. The architect took umbrage, and the ensuing feud raged on for days to the delight of the "in" group of Romans. Bernini proceeded with his work, but arranged the four central figures of the fountain in such a way that two of them stand forever with their backs to the church, another has her long hair combed down over her face so that she cannot see the offending edifice, while the fourth is thumbing his nose in the classic gesture at the still-standing dome.

The BAULETTO CON FUNGHI is also outstanding at Tre Scalini. These veal-birds are served everywhere in Italy, but the chef here has brought his far out of the realm of the ordinary.

To prepare these for 6 guests, you will need:

12 medium-size veal cutlets—flattened very thin
36 mushrooms
1 clove garlic, minced
1 cup chopped parsley
½ teaspoon rosemary (ground)
½ teaspoon salt
½ teaspoon black pepper
¼ pound butter
½ cup heavy cream
1 cup bread crumbs
½ cup Marsala wine
2 egg yolks
juice of 1 lemon

Chop the funghi and sauté in butter and olive oil to which you have added a minced clove of garlic, chopped parsley, ½ teaspoon of ground rosemary, salt, and pepper. Remove from the fire and add 1 cup of bread crumbs and enough Marsala to moisten the mixture. Place 2 tablespoons of the filling on each cutlet, roll up tightly and fasten with skewers. Sauté in a heavy skillet in butter, cover the pan and cook for 15 minutes. Remove "birds" and to the pan-juices add the ½ cup of cream and the Marsala mixed with the egg yolks. Stir, and when slightly thickened, remove from the fire and add the lemon juice. Pour over the 12 birds, and serve with gnocchi which has been baked with a coating of butter and Parmesan.

A trip to Capri is in no way complete without a

visit to La Canzone del Mare at Piccolo Marina. This ristorante is owned by Gracie Fields, the famous English singer and comedienne, and the setting is truly the most exotic one can ever encounter; the ambiance that of a gracious hostess entertaining only you at her private villa.

This is exactly what the place was originally when Miss Fields found it as a retreat, but now she generously shares it, and how fortunate for us. The food and service are vastly superior to anything you will find elsewhere on this enchanted island. I urge you to have seafood, and whatever you select, rest assured it was swimming that morning in the blue waters that you are sitting beside while you dine.

At La Canzone del Mare the SAUTÉED MEDITERRANEAN PERCH is dusted with flour before sautéing in a heavy skillet in butter and olive oil seasoned with salt and pepper. Brown the fish on both sides, then add a minced clove of garlic, a cup of minced parsley and a small can of peeled tomatoes. Cover and cook for about 15 minutes. Then add a few well-scrubbed mussels and cook until the shells open.

Almost any fish can be cooked this way—cod, halibut, or mackerel.

One of the really authoritative cooking guides describes MIRONTON DE BOEUF as a stew made with cooked meat, and I bow to their prescience. My version of Mironton is far different, and perhaps it should be re-christened. By any other name, however, it would still be delicious, and to quote my

143

favorite playwright, "What's in a name?"

For 6 servings you will need:

3 pounds lean chuck beef (cut into 1-inch cubes)
1 pound onions (peeled and chopped)
6 cloves garlic (sliced)
6 shallots (sliced)
2 bay leaves
1 dozen whole peppercorns
6 whole cloves
3 cups dry red wine
3 cups canned beef consommé
3 tablespoons flour

Place the cubes of meat in an enamel pot and add the onions, garlic, shallots, bay leaves, peppercorns, and cloves. Mix the 3 cups of red wine with the 3 cups of consommé and pour over the meat. Cover the pot and refrigerate for 24 hours.

Then, strain off the marinade and reserve. Sauté the meat and onions in butter and olive oil, and place in a flame-proof casserole. Add 3 tablespoons of flour to the oil and butter, and stir to blend. Heat the marinade and add to this roux, cooking until thickened. Add ½ cup of Kitchen Bouquet for color, if desired. Pour over the meat. Put the lid on the casserole and cook over a medium heat 2½ hours or until the meat is fork-tender. Serve with cooked noodles to which you have added sour cream and chopped chives—1 cup of sour cream to 4 cups of noodles. The perfect vegetable accompaniment is rutabagas—the much-neglected member of the turnip fam-

Beef a' La Matador if
Corn meal dumplings

ily. Peel and dice them, boil gently in sufficient water to cover, to which you have added salt and sugar to taste. Drain and add butter. Delicious!

I recently had an experience in helping to open a brand-new restaurant which has a Mexican motif in décor. I created a dish which became a tremendous success, and naturally this delighted me—BEEF À LA MATADOR.

I used 1-inch cubes of beef and for 6 servings I suggest 3 pounds. Place the meat in a Dutch oven and add 3 heaping tablespoons of flour, stirring well to coat each piece.

Sauté the meat until slightly browned; then add the following:

> *1 cup concentrated frozen orange juice*
> *2 cups dry sherry*
> *3 tablespoons of Kitchen Bouquet*
> *2 teaspoons salt*
> *1 teaspoon white pepper*
> *2 crumbled bay leaves*
> *4 medium-size onions, chopped*
> *3 stalks celery cut into 1-inch pieces*
> *6 whole cloves*
> *6 juniper berries*
> *2 oranges cut up—rind and all*

Cover and cook over a medium heat about 2½ hours, or until meat is fork-tender.

To prepare CORNMEAL DUMPLINGS for 6, use 2 cups *Dumpling* of flour, 1 cup of yellow cornmeal, 2 teaspoons of bak- *Cornmeal* ing powder, ½ teaspoon of salt, 1 egg, 1 cup of milk,

145

Corn dumplings

and 4 tablespoons of melted butter. Mix together, allow dough to rest 5 minutes, then drop by spoonfuls onto the top of the stew. Cover and cook gently for 15 minutes. Serve with a garnish of preserved kumquats and whole pimientos.

Another creation which I did for this restaurant I call EGGS SAN DIEGO.

For 8 servings you will need:

> *1 avocado, peeled and cut up*
> *2 cloves garlic*
> *½ cucumber, peeled*
> *1 teaspoon salt*
> *1 teaspoon chili powder*
> *juice of two lemons*
> *Tabasco*
> *1 cup finely minced clams*
> *a few leaves chopped lettuce*
> *8 eggs, hard-boiled*
> *a few teaspoons chives, chopped*
> *8 ripe olives, pitted*

Make a Guacamole by placing in a blender the avocado, garlic, cucumber, salt, chili powder, lemon juice, and a few drops of Tabasco. Blend on high speed. Remove from blender and stir in the clams. Chill for 3 or 4 hours. To serve: place chopped lettuce in a stemmed sherbet glass, and on this place 1 sliced hard-boiled egg. Cover with the sauce, sprinkle with chopped chives and in the center place a pitted ripe olive. This is an excellent appetizer, and when you serve it you may forget the salad course with the meal.

The famous Colony Restaurant in New York frequently features on their summer luncheon buffet COLD CURRIED CHICKEN, which is far, far more delicious than it may sound. I have copied this, and whenever I serve it the guests' reactions are well worth the effort. I have come to use only the breasts of chicken, as they look better and the portions are uniform. I boil 4 whole breasts (split in half and partially boned out) in chicken consommé to which I add a generous amount of curry powder and 2 chopped apples, 2 chopped onions, and 1 cup of chopped celery. I use the hot variety of curry powder, but suit yourself. Just don't be stingy with it.

When the chicken is tender, remove it from the pot and allow to cool in a rather deep dish. Boil the broth and thicken it with flour and butter, well blended together and dropped into the stock in small bits. Stir until thickened, then remove from the fire and add 1 cup of cream. Strain over the chicken breasts and when cool, refrigerate overnight. Serve with cold cooked rice (use the pre-cooked variety, as the grains stay separate and it is not gooey with starch) to which you have added small white seeded raisins and chopped parsley. Of course Major Grey's Chutney is very much in order, and pass along with it chopped cucumber, toasted slivers of almonds, crumbled bacon, and grated toasted coconut. This is wonderful for a Sunday lunch for 4 in summer, for all the work has been done the day before and you have time to spray the roses or mow the lawn before the guests arrive. To make life even more relaxed, serve a simple dessert such as orange ice with Mandarin orange sections (canned) over which you pour Curaçao.

As of right now, start saving those small quantities of leftover meats that you usually keep for 3 days in the refrigerator and then give to the dog. Put them in a plastic bag and keep in the freezer. Save everything, whatever it is—scraps of roast, those 2 sausages that were left at breakfast, calf's liver, beef stew, chicken. I don't need to list these: just save everything, except the bones.

When you have accumulated 4 pounds, invite 8 guests for Sunday-night supper and serve Eggs Polonaise.

Grind your cache of tidbits, using the medium blade of your meat grinder. Also grind and add 3 peeled onions, 6 shallots, and 2 or 3 cloves of garlic. Stir in 2 cups of tomato purée and 1 cup of red wine. Salt to taste. Place in a heavy pan over a low heat, cover, and cook for about 1 hour, stirring frequently.

Now poach 2 eggs per guest in boiling water to which you have added a generous splash of vinegar and salt to taste.

Place the meat on a heated platter in a flat mound, patting it gently with the flat side of a large spoon. Arrange the poached eggs on top, working quickly so they will not get cold.

Have ready a cup of melted butter to which you

have added 2 tablespoons of very fine bread crumbs and 1 teaspoon of paprika. Put a spoonful of this over each egg. Sprinkle freshly chopped parsley over all, and stand back ready to blush while the guests ooh and aah over your Eggs Polonaise.

Of course a salad is very much in order as an accompaniment, so I hope you had the foresight to plant some nasturtiums on the first warm day of spring. They thrive anywhere in any soil and need no attention. Don't worry. They'll grow. Come July and the guests have arrived for a festive weekend. This particular group is so salad-prone that most of them dote on every corner health-food store from the good one at 57th Street and Seventh Avenue in Manhattan to the really kookie ones in southern California.

It's off-season for endive, and the brook watercress has sort of overdeveloped. So, for these guests gather the new nasturtium leaves (nasturtiums grow very fast, so there are always new leaves) and a few blossoms for color. Wash them well in ice water. After snipping with the shears into thin strips, add the leaves to the salad bowl along with the Boston lettuce and the white part of chicory. Toss with your favorite French dressing. Place the blossoms on top, and the salad is ready to serve.

Speaking of salads, the often-discredited WALDORF SALAD makes an ideal summer luncheon. Use 1 cup each of diced celery hearts, crisp apples diced, and slivered almonds, all mixed with 4 tablespoons of mayonnaise to which is added the juice of 1 lemon.

Left over salad w/ chicken on bread slice
Bananas & chutney on lettuce
Cukes w/ dill vinegar

Off the Top of My Range

Not only is this good for lunch, it isn't a bad idea
at all on a cold winter evening when you don't feel
you can possibly cope with fixing a TV dinner.

If you have any leftover Waldorf Salad, you can
always "goose it up" for lunch tomorrow. Add 1
cup of diced chicken to each cup of salad, and an
additional ½ cup of mayonnaise, into which you
have blended a heaping teaspoon of curry powder.
Spread the mixture on buttered bread, topping each
with another slice of buttered bread. Cut in quarters
after trimming the crusts. Sliced cucumbers with
dill-flavored vinegar make an ideal accompaniment.
If your cucumbers are not ready to pick, settle for
sliced bananas mixed with Major Grey's Chutney.
For each cup of bananas use 2 tablespoons of chutney and a dash of lemon juice. Serve on a bed of
chicory.

While we are still in the sandwich mood, why not
make some open-face CURRIED-EGG SANDWICHES?
Boil 6 eggs, using a 2-quart pot and cold water.
Place over a medium heat, adding a tablespoon of
salt to the water. When it starts to boil, time it for 5
minutes. Remove from fire, drain, and fill the pot
with cold water. Shell the eggs. Chop them
medium-fine, add 1 cup of finely chopped celery and
a tablespoon of curry powder. Salt to taste. Arrange
the mixture on large rounds of buttered bread, and
sprinkle with toasted sesame seeds. Very crisp sweet
pickles are ideal with these.

As delectable as CROQUES MONSIEUR are, don't
plan to serve them at your next bridge luncheon, as

they must be eaten the minute they are ready. Serve something else. But I suspect you'll think of an occasion when they will fit in perfectly.

The purpose of this book is to suggest ideas; *not* to arrange your life. Anyway, whenever you think is the proper moment, be sure you have cold sliced ham, Swiss cheese (not the kind from those mountains of Wisconsin but from those other high mountains), and this cheese also must be sliced. You will need sliced bread, but unbuttered this time. Place a slice of cheese on a slice of bread, add a slice of ham, another slice of cheese, and top with a slice of bread. Let's assume you are making 6. In that case break 2 eggs into a bowl, beat slightly with a fork, salt to taste, a sprinkle of white pepper, and add 1 cup of milk. Dip each sandwich into this batter and sauté in butter, turning once. It should take about 3 minutes for each side. I like them with plum jam and English mustard—that marvelous combination served in Chinese restaurants. If there is not a Chinese supermarket near you, try mixing 2 teaspoons of Coleman's Dry Mustard with enough cold water to make a thin paste, then stir in ½ cup of jelly. Almost any kind will do, except grape.

Many cooks I know neglect seafood for one reason or another, yet there are so many interesting things one can do with fruits de mer that convince everyone you are a gourmet cook. For example, to prepare what I call Shrimp Key Largo, buy some large raw shrimp, allowing 6 shrimp per person. Peel them, leaving the tail intact, de-vein them with a small sharp knife, rinse them with cold water, and dry on paper towels. Also have ready some large fresh mushroom caps (save the stems as we have a place for them later).

Now cook some wild rice. I cook mine in chicken consommé with a generous amount of butter added.

Melt ½ pound of oleomargarine in a heavy skillet and add 3 slivered cloves of garlic. In this, sauté the shrimp for about 5 minutes, turning frequently. Remove the shrimp and keep them hot in the oven, while you sauté the mushroom caps in the same pan. Do not overcook them; they are tender and really require a minimum of cooking.

Chop the mushroom stems and sauté them quickly in butter. Add them to the hot wild rice, which you then put onto a heated platter, arrange the shrimps and mushrooms over the rice, sprinkle with fresh tarragon, and serve.

With it pass a mixed green salad (lettuce, watercress, and fresh spinach make a good mixture). The SUMMER SALAD DRESSING: mix 1 cup of honey, 2 cups of cider vinegar, 1 teaspoon of garlic powder, 2 teaspoons of salt, 1 teaspoon of ground black pepper, 2 egg whites, 1 tablespoon of dry mustard, and 1 tablespoon of chopped fresh or dried basil. Put into the blender—high speed for 1 minute. Toast 1 cup of sesame seeds spread out in a pie plate in the oven set at 300°F. for about 10 minutes or until slightly brown. Sprinkle these over the portions of salad. This dressing is also an excellent topping for fresh fruit salad, or on sliced tomatoes.

Fresh lobster is a great favorite with many Americans, but most people prefer to go to a seafood restaurant whenever the lobster urge comes over them. Perhaps it is because lobsters must be cooked alive, which is not a pleasant thought. Those who do prepare lobster at home usually boil it in gallons of plain tap water, not realizing it should be done in a minimum of water to which white wine and a bouquet garni have been added. The pot should have a tight-fitting lid so that the lobsters steam rather than boil. Small lobsters should cook only until the shells turn red, larger ones 5 minutes longer. Too much cooking toughens the meat.

Broiling is something else, and should be done only by an experienced cook—and the best way is over charcoal on the outdoor grill. The lobsters must be split lengthwise (the craw removed), generously buttered, broiled quickly, and eaten immediately.

There is a much simpler way to enjoy this delicacy at home. To prepare LOBSTER À LA NEWBURG, I buy the fresh frozen Canadian lobster meat, most of which is prepared in Nova Scotia. A 14-ounce can holds sufficient lobster to serve 2 if the meat is sautéed in butter and no sauce is added.

However, for 4 guests, do it spectacularly in this fashion. Defrost 2 cans of the lobster meat and cut it into pieces. Sauté in butter in a chafing dish at the table. Pour in a generous amount of brandy and ignite. When the flames die down, have ready the following NEWBURG SAUCE.

Make a roux using ¼ pound of butter and 2 tablespoons of flour. Stir over a low flame to blend well and cook the flour. Add 1 cup of milk (hot) and 1 cup of cream. Stir until thickened. Beat 2 egg yolks and to them add a few spoonfuls of the hot sauce. Stir together and add to the remaining sauce. Do not boil it now, as the eggs might curdle, but keep over a low flame and stir. Remove from the fire and add ½ cup of dry sherry, a liberal sprinkling of nutmeg, and a pinch of salt.

Pour this sauce over the sautéed lobster, stir gently to blend, and serve on saffron rice or toast points.

PURÉE OF PEAS DUCHESSE is an excellent accompaniment. For 4 persons, cook 1 quart of freshly shelled peas in a small amount of boiling water for 6 minutes, and drain. Rub the cooked peas through a sieve, season with salt and pepper and a tablespoon of butter. Add 2 egg yolks and stir well. With a pastry bag, make mounds of the peas on a well-greased cookie sheet, and place in the oven set at 300°F. for no more than 10 minutes.

To make ARTICHAUDS CLAMART, proceed exactly as above except put the purée of peas in mounds on artichoke bottoms.

If you want a change of pace, why not try these TIDEWATER CRAB CAKES? You will need for 6 servings:

1½ pounds backfin crabmeat
    or 1½ pounds Alaskan King Crabmeat
8 slices of bread

¼ pound melted butter
3 egg yolks (beaten)
1 tablespoon dry mustard
½ teaspoon salt
Worcestershire sauce
3 egg whites (beaten)

Pick over the crabmeat to remove any bits of shell. Trim the crusts from the bread and cut the bread into small cubes. Place in a bowl, pour the melted butter over, and toss to coat the bread. Now add the beaten egg yolks, mixed with the dry mustard, salt, and a tablespoon of Worcestershire sauce. Mix well and add the crabmeat. Beat the egg whites until stiff and fold into the mixture. Shape into 8 patties and sauté in butter until brown on both sides. Serve with a rich cream sauce to which you have added 1 or 2 chopped hard-boiled eggs.

With this I like to serve RAW FRIED POTATOES. Peel 6 medium-size potatoes and grate them on the coarsest side of the grater. Cover with ice water for at least ½ hour. When ready to cook them, drain in a colander, then place in a heavy towel and wring them until dry. Heat bacon fat or chicken fat in a heavy skillet, add the grated potatoes, and sprinkle with salt and pepper. Cook over a medium heat for 10 minutes (or until well browned). Then turn carefully with a wide spatula and cook 10 minutes longer.

FILET OF SOLE MARGUERY is really very easy to prepare, and if you serve it your guests will assume you have studied cooking in Paris, France.

Make a fish stock by boiling the fish heads and bones in half water and half white wine, to which you add ½ bay leaf, salt, pepper, 2 shallots, and 1 small onion. Strain and reserve.

Also, steam 2 dozen mussels; strain and reserve the liquor. If mussels are not easily obtainable, and often they are not, I substitute oysters.

Mix the fish stock and the mussel liquor in a shallow pan and bring to a rolling boil. In this poach the 8 portions of filet of sole (or flounder) for 5 minutes. Remove the fish with a skimmer, and arrange in a flat baking dish which is liberally coated with sweet butter.

Slice a dozen large mushrooms and boil them quickly in a small amount of water and lemon juice, salted to taste. Drain and reserve.

Now combine all 3 liquids and boil to reduce to about 2 cups. Add ½ cup of white wine and ½ teaspoon of thyme. Beat 3 egg yolks and stir into this, and bring to a boil, stirring constantly. Remove from the fire and add ½ cup of heavy cream.

Arrange the sliced mushrooms, the mussels, and a dozen or so small cooked shrimp on the filets. Pour the hot sauce over all and place under the broiler for 5 minutes. Serve at once.

⌁ VI ⌁

DESSERTS AND OTHER
AFTERTHOUGHTS

Harper's Bazaar used to feature a column each
month called "Why Don't You?" which was so in-
triguing and "in" at that time that the famous
Spivy even did a song called "Why Don't You?" at
her popular penthouse supper club. To this day I
recall several of the lyrics, one line of which was
"Why don't you dip your head in brandy and light
it?"

Instead, why don't you . . .

Keep three or four orange-chiffon cakes in your
freezer? Make them if you must, but it is far easier
(and much less costly) just to buy the commercial
ones at the good ole A&P, or wherever you market.

Defrost one of the cakes (it takes about 2 hours at
room temperature) and slice it into 3 layers crosswise. Having put the bottom layer on your best cake
plate, douse it generously with dark rum, then carefully spread defrozen orange juice over it. Add
layer number 2 and treat it the same way, working
fast so the orange juice won't melt too much. After
you have put the top layer in place, ice the entire

cake with flavored whipped cream. (To 1 pint of heavy cream add 2 tablespoons of instant coffee while beating, gradually adding ¾ cup of superfine granulated sugar.) Chill the cake in the refrigerator, and serve with coffee ice cream. Or, omit the ice cream and allow the guests "seconds" of the JAMAICA ORANGE CAKE.

Or . . . Proceed in the same manner as above, replacing the orange juice on layer number 1 with chocolate filling (use the packaged kind, but add a square of bitter chocolate while cooking). On layer number 2, spread vanilla custard (again, the packaged kind), then ice over-all with whipped cream flavored with brandy instead of instant coffee. With this version, use white rum instead of dark, as it will blend more felicitously with the chocolate and vanilla. Result: RUM CAKE SUPREME.

You could wait until the next Strawberry Festival and substitute Curaçao or Triple Sec for the rum, and sliced fresh strawberries (which you have sweetened with confectioner's sugar) for the orange juice. This time flavor the whipped cream with Curaçao or Triple Sec, depending on which you have used for the layers, and garnish the entire outside of the cake with strawberries cut in half. STRAWBERRY SHORTCAKE, unheard of by Fanny Farmer.

These cakes are proof that there is nothing new under the sun, since each is just a variation of the famous Italian Zuppa Inglese. And who but the Italians would christen their celebrated dessert "English Soup"?

When in a Gallic mood, whip up one of these chiffon cakes into a GÂTEAU BEURRE AU CAFÉ. Use ½ pound of sweet (unsalted) butter which has been taken out of the refrigerator at least 1 hour in advance. Place the butter in a bowl, and with your fingers work into it 2 raw egg yolks, and ½ cup of superfine granulated sugar mixed with 3 tablespoons of instant coffee. I use Italian espresso, but you may feel safer with regular instant as not everyone likes the stronger variety. This time cut the cake into 2 layers instead of 3. Between the layers you may use either this Beurre-au-Café mixture or a custard flavored with almond extract. Then ice the entire cake with the Beurre au Café and roll it in slivered almonds which you have toasted in the oven on a cookie sheet. Place the gâteau on your favorite cake plate and cover the top with more toasted almonds (about ¾ cup) chopped very fine. Chill at least 2 hours in the refrigerator. Cut with a dull knife . . . then if a fight starts over the last piece, there will be no dangerous weapons at hand.

Why not make a CHOCOLATE ROLL, especially if you are the show-off type?

First, check and see if you have any Dutch-process cocoa (the real thing, please; not the kind made somewhere in Pennsylvania). If you don't have any, and the stores are closed, wait until you are able to acquire some.

Put 5 tablespoons of the cocoa in a flour sifter together with 1 cup of confectioner's sugar and 4 tablespoons (level) of flour. Sift into a mixing bowl.

Now separate 6 large eggs, beating the yolks until creamy and adding to them 1 tablespoon of vanilla. Beat the whites at high speed until very stiff, adding ½ teaspoon of cream of tartar while beating.

Blend the beaten yolks and the dry mixture into the whites all at one time, preferably with a rubber spatula. Work gently but thoroughly.

Pour the mixture onto a jelly-roll pan which you have first greased, then lined with waxed paper. Bake for 15 minutes at 350°F.

Have ready a dampened tea towel, and invert the cake pan onto it as soon as you take it from the oven. Carefully remove the waxed paper and gently roll the cake into the towel. Allow to cool for 20 minutes. Unroll and spread with a pint of heavy cream which you have whipped until stiff and to which you have added ¾ cup of superfine granulated sugar and ¼ cup of your best brandy.

Again roll up the cake. This time omit the towel. I mention this as I know a newlywed who made her first Jelly Roll and included in the final roll-up one of the hemstitched towels from her trousseau!

Spread the outside of the roll with more whipped cream, covering it completely—including the ends. Have a square of bittersweet chocolate at room temperature, and, using a vegetable peeler, make curls of the chocolate over the top of the roll. Chill thoroughly in the refrigerator. And why don't you . . . keep off those scales?

If the day is cold and the guests expect you to show off your culinary prowess, serve a dessert which I once enjoyed at the home of David Kidd, the well-known designer. This recipe for BEIGNETS WITH APRICOT SAUCE is from David's private file.

In a heavy saucepan melt ¼ pound of sweet butter in 1 cup of water. When it is melted and the water starts to boil, add 1 cup of flour, ¼ cup of sugar, and ¼ teaspoon of salt all at once. Stir until the dough leaves the sides of the pan and forms a ball. Then remove from the fire and cool for 5 minutes. Now stir in (one at a time) 4 eggs. Beat well. Place in refrigerator until ready to use.

Ten minutes before you are ready to serve dinner (or lunch, as the case may be), melt 2 pounds of Crisco in a heavy saucepan. Heat until a cube of bread browns at once when dropped into the fat.

Drop the dough by soupspoonfuls into the hot Crisco and fry until well browned. Do 4 or 5 at a time so the fat does not cool off. Remove to a pan which you have lined with paper towels, and keep hot in the oven (200°F.).

Meanwhile, melt 1 jar of apricot preserves with 3 tablespoons of water and ⅛ pound of butter. When heated, stir in ½ cup of apricot brandy and keep hot in a double-boiler. Serve 3 or 4 beignets to each of your 6 guests. Pass the sauce in a heated sauceboat.

Speaking of apricots brings to mind quince. Have you ever tried to find a recipe for quince jelly, quince jam, or quince preserves in your collection of cookbooks? Forget it.

Today someone stopped by and left a dozen quinces for me, and my immediate reaction was

161

"Now what?" I'm fond of QUINCE JELLY, but somehow had always let Crosse & Blackwell worry about making it for me.

I probably have many more cookbooks than most people, but rather than count them I shall just report that it takes about two hours to look in the indexes for "quince." Frustrated but undaunted I just peeled the luscious-smelling fruit, cored and quartered them, and then cut them into small pieces. These I placed in a heavy kettle and added just enough cold water to cover. As an afterthought, I squeezed the juice of 2 lemons into the pot and cooked the quinces for 30 minutes. Then I lowered the fire to medium, stirred in 2 pounds of granulated sugar, and cooked another hour. (Naturally the cooking time depends on the degree of ripeness of the fruit, so test for doneness.) I added 1 cup of Certo and removed from heat, then poured it into glasses of various sizes—small ones for guests' breakfast trays, and larger ones for table use.

Marion Mill Preminger, when she reigned as Hollywood's leading hostess, created a dessert for a luncheon-party she once gave in honor of Lady Mendl. Determined to outdo herself as an ingenious menu planner, Marion bought small clay flower pots and in the bottom of each she placed a thin chocolate mint. She filled each pot with vanilla ice cream, then dusted the top with a thin layer of cocoa. Picking some of her choice anemones (any flowers will do), she wrapped the stems with foil and inserted them into the center of the ice cream. POT DE FLEURS

MARION. Simple, but extremely effective, especially for a luncheon you are giving for a bride-to-be or your garden club.

If you have youngsters who like to cook but you are annoyed by the havoc they create in the kitchen, then by all means let them try this dessert, called WAIKIKI PUDDING. They'll love it, and so will you.

Place an unopened can of condensed milk (the sweetened kind) in a pot of water. Boil it, uncovered, over a medium heat for 3 hours. Replace the water as it boils away so that the can is completely covered the entire time. Cool and refrigerate for at least 12 hours. (Several of these can be boiled at one time as they will keep indefinitely if unopened.)

The result will delight you, if you are a caramel lover, for this process produces an excellent, creamy-soft confection. Serve it by placing a tablespoon of the caramel in a sherbet glass. Fill the glass with chilled, crushed pineapple; top with whipped cream and sprinkle with crushed toasted almonds. One can will serve ten people.

Verna Wood, our local assistant postmistress, told me recently about a cake she has invented. Verna calls this APPLE SURPRISE. To make it she uses 1 jar of spiced apple-rings and a box of prepared Apple-Spice cake mix. She drains the apple-rings, then arranges them in the bottom of a well-buttered oblong cake pan. The cake mix is prepared according to directions on the carton and poured carefully over the apple rings. It is baked for 30 minutes in a 375°F. oven, cooled on a rack for 10 minutes, and then inverted onto a platter. With this Verna passes a bowl of whipped cream sweetened with granulated brown sugar and flavored with a generous teaspoon of cinnamon. It is especially good as a dessert for Sunday brunch.

No matter what you are serving, the presentation is as important as the preparation. Not only should the servings have eye appeal (and please do not make the portions too large), but the table setting and its centerpiece should be in keeping with the occasion and the menu.

When desperate for a centerpiece and the florist shops are closed, the garden bare, not even a late-blooming dandelion in sight, indeed even the greenhouse is bare, and 6 guests are coming for dinner . . . why don't you scrub 6 or 8 Idaho potatoes, arrange them in the center of your bare, highly-polished table, and then unclasp your pearls—the ones Uncle Nat brought back from Osaka—and drape them artistically over and around and about the Pearls of Idaho? Voilà, Pearlie Mae.

If you dare, wash a fairly large piece of cannel coal and set it in the center of your table. Then, with clear Scotch tape, fasten two or three gardenias, or other exotic flowers of your choice, to the coal. Simple, sophisticated, and extremely effective.

My friend Kay Walter, who now lives in Palm Beach, is married to a White Russian, Serge Walter, whose father was the former mayor of Petrograd. An extremely gifted painter, Kay decorates eggs each Easter in such a baroque manner that they look like gifts for Catherine the Great. Arranged in a shallow basket (sprayed with gold), they create a centerpiece for an Easter brunch which would lift even a mundane meal into the realms of sheer elegance.

By the same token, a basket lined with evergreens and then filled with elaborate Christmas-tree ornaments is perfect for a December 25 gathering of the clan.

At a Writers' Group luncheon, the centerpieces were antique inkwells, each containing an arrangement of dark red sweetheart roses. These caused favorable comments even from the male guests.

At one Bar-Mitzvah dinner held at the Ambassador Hotel, the theme was chemistry, since the guest of honor was "hooked" on the subject. The centerpieces were groups of beakers of various sizes and shapes from a laboratory-supply house. Filled with colored water and lighted by concealed votive candles, they were extremely effective.

Patricia Easterbrook Roberts, who now lives in Connecticut, has had an enviable career which started in Sydney, Australia, where at an early age she opened a flower shop. Soon her reputation for ingenious creativity came to the attention of Constance Spry in London. Pat was summoned by the formidable Miss Spry and immediately taken on as her number-one assistant. When the time came to open a branch shop in New York, it was Miss Easterbrook who was given the assignment. Now my gifted friend spends part of each year in Italy de-

signing flowers executed in metal by a family in one
of the remote hill towns, where their forge is kept
aglow turning out her creations. In Connecticut, Pat
idles away her time writing books on flowers and
how to arrange them, table settings, and decorations
for every occasion. I asked her to share with us a
few of her non-floral ideas for the despairing hostess, such as:

For festive days like New Year's, hang or clip
earrings onto bare branches (high-bush blueberry is
feathery and good form). Impale the stem into a
florist's pin holder, which can be covered with a
necklace or two.

Or, red clay flower pots filled with green grapes
and limes, arranged on house bricks that overlap to
form steps.

Or, fill two or three hurricane globes with
fruit—mixed—or all one kind, such as cherries,
strawberries, grapes, etc.

Or, why not use your own imagination—which I
hope I have kindled by now—and come up with
something original and truly yours?

Ah, "truly yours" is perhaps as fitting an ending
as any to these tales of cookery. For I have traveled
an interesting gastronomic route since those happy,
carefree days when I could eat 3 biscuit halves in
fricassee gravy before Grandfather served the rest
of the family. And I shall be forever beholden to
Hettie for kindling my interest in food. She would
never understand Escargots, Riz de Veau, Ani-
melles de Mouton Frites, Grenouilles Sautées à la

Provençale, or Tripe à la Mode de Caen, but she inspired, unknowingly, a young boy's interest in the goodness of victuals.

For this I am eternally grateful. Merci beaucoup, ma chère Hettie.

INDEX

MAURICE BROCKWAY

Maurice Brockway grew up in upstate New York in a small American town a few miles from the Canadian border, in a rambling white house where cooking and eating were given their proper reverence. After college (Ithaca) and a few years in the business world of New York City, he bought an old inn in Stamford, Connecticut, and operated it as Brockton Manor for several years during the 1940's.

Then he was appointed assistant banquet manager of the Hotel Plaza in New York, and later became director of sales and catering manager of the Ambassador Hotel, staying on when it became the Sheraton-East.

He has a talent for being able to "cook by ear," and can duplicate any dish he has eaten anywhere in the world. This lifelong interest in food is reflected in the nostalgic quality of *Come Cook with Me,* his narrative about the pleasures of cooking and eating.

A few years ago, Mr. Brockway bought and restored a 200-year-old mill house in Bucks County, where he now lives.